It's TIME

Themes and Imperatives for Mathematics Education

A LEADERSHIP FRAMEWORK FOR COMMON CORE MATHEMATICS

LEADERSHIP IN MATHEMATICS EDUCATION

NCSM
NETWORK
COMMUNICATE
SUPPORT
MOTIVATE

Solution Tree | Press

a division of
Solution Tree

Published by Solution Tree Press
555 North Morton Street
Bloomington, IN 47404
800.733.6786 (toll free) / 812.336.7700
FAX: 812.336.7790

email: info@solution-tree.com
solution-tree.com
Visit **go.solution-tree.com/mathematics** to access materials related to this book.
Printed in the United States of America

18 17 16 15 14   1 2 3 4 5

Library of Congress Cataloging-in-Publication Data

It's TIME : Themes and Imperatives for Mathematics Education / [by National Council of Supervisors of Mathematics].
        pages cm
  Includes bibliographical references and index.
   ISBN 978-1-936764-91-4 (perfect bound) 1. Mathematics--Study and teaching. 2. Individualized instruction. 3. Effective teaching. 4. Leadership. I. National Council of Supervisors of Mathematics. II. Title: Themes and Imperatives for Mathematics Education. III. Title: It is TIME.
  QA20.I53I87 2014
  510.71'073--dc23
                        2014000422

Solution Tree
Jeffrey C. Jones, CEO
Edmund M. Ackerman, President

Solution Tree Press
President: Douglas M. Rife
Editorial Director: Lesley Bolton
Managing Production Editor: Caroline Weiss
Production Editor: Tara Perkins
Copy Editor: Sarah Payne-Mills
Proofreader: Elisabeth Abrams
Text and Cover Designer: Rian Anderson

Acknowledgments

It's TIME: Themes and Imperatives for Mathematics Education is the result of the strategic planning of the National Council of Supervisors of Mathematics (NCSM) Board of Directors, conducted at its summer 2011 leadership meeting. With the support of then president Suzanne Mitchell and board members, NCSM began two years of intensively thinking, reflecting, researching, and writing about a simple question with a complex answer: What leadership imperatives are essential so that all students benefit from the Common Core State Standards for mathematics (CCSSM)?

During the two-year journey, the writers built upon the hallmark document *The PRIME Leadership Framework: Principles and Indicators for Mathematics Education Leaders* (NCSM, 2008). They considered conditions needed to support mathematics instruction, including shifting the beliefs and mindsets of designated leaders, maximizing opportunity for all students to learn, maximizing instructional capacity in every classroom, and developing collaborative structures and productive cultures so that teachers have the opportunity to grow in their understanding of mathematics and how best to teach it. To address the complex issues inherent in the leadership imperatives, the NCSM Board commissioned a diverse writing team. The team, led by Steve Leinwand, worked throughout 2012 and 2013. The writing team members included Don Balka, Vanessa Cleaver, Lynn Columba, Linda Fulmore, Ted Hull, Tim Kanold, Ruth Miles, Valerie Mills, Suzanne Mitchell, Kit Norris, Kathy Ross, Steve Viktora, Charles Watson, and Gwen Zimmermann. The board is extremely grateful to each of these NCSM members for his or her dedication, time, energy, and effort to research and write the themes and imperatives for mathematics education. This book moved from idea to reality because of the writers' wisdom, experience, and insight.

The board also wishes to extend sincere thanks to the many organizations and individuals in the educational community who willingly contributed and responded to drafts of *It's TIME* in 2013. NCSM is indebted to the many individuals who responded with deep understanding and input that significantly shaped the final document. These primary reviewers include past NCSM presidents and mathematics leaders Diane Briars, Carol Edwards, Shirley Frye, Carol Greenes, and Henry Kepner.

The 2012–2014 NCSM Boards of Directors reviewed and endorsed the mathematics imperatives identified in this book during the summer of 2013. The members' wisdom, insight, and feedback were essential to the final development of the imperatives. NCSM extends special thanks to board members Wanda Audrict, Hope Bjerke, Laura Godrey, Linda Griffith, Ted Hull, Diana Kendrick, Suzanne Libfeld, Carol Matsumoto, Valerie Mills, Eric Milou, Suzanne Mitchell, Mari Muri, Kathy Rieke, Connie Schrock, Mona Toncheff, Steve Viktora, and Gwen Zimmermann for their extensive feedback throughout the development process.

We would especially like to thank chief editor Steve Leinwand for his expertise, guidance, and support throughout the many drafts. His work and contribution were essential to the project.

We also wish to thank the professional staff at Solution Tree for their invaluable assistance. We thank Tara Perkins at Solution Tree for her patient spirit, positive attitude, and desire to make this document a reality for mathematics leaders.

Finally, thanks to our families. NCSM is an organization of volunteers who have a passion for leadership—volunteers who are supported by those they love in order to do the work that is their passion. On behalf of the writers and reviewers of *It's TIME*, we thank you.

—Valerie Mills, President of NCSM (2013–2015)

—Suzanne Mitchell, President of NCSM (2011–2013)

Visit **go.solution-tree.com/mathematics**
to access materials related to this book.

Table of Contents

■ ■ ■ ■

Reproducible pages are in italics.

About the National Council of Supervisors of Mathematics

■ ■ ■ ■

The National Council of Supervisors of Mathematics (NCSM) is an international leadership organization for those who serve the NCSM vision of excellence and equity for student achievement in mathematics. NCSM is founded on the strength and dedication of a growing membership of mathematics education leaders. These leaders include grade-level team leaders, course-level team leaders, department chairs, district or county coaches and coordinators, site-based teacher leaders, district or provincial curriculum directors, principals, superintendents, college faculty and trainers of teacher leaders, and all who work to ensure the success of every mathematics student.

NCSM was created at the 1968 Philadelphia meeting of the National Council of Teachers of Mathematics (NCTM) when a group of urban district supervisors decided that at the next annual meeting (Minneapolis, 1969) school district leaders should gather to form the National Council of Supervisors of Mathematics to address leadership issues in mathematics. An early and critical issue for NCSM was defining the membership. The founding members chose *not* to restrict membership to supervisors and instead welcomed all leaders and teachers of mathematics. The open-membership theme has continued throughout the years; the thirty-five leaders who attended that first meeting in Minneapolis grew to more than three thousand by the end of the 20th century.

As NCSM celebrates its forty-sixth anniversary in 2014, the vision and ideals of our founders endure.

> **N—Network** and collaborate with stakeholders in education, business, and government communities to ensure the growth and development of mathematics education leaders.

> **C—Communicate** current and relevant research to mathematics leaders, and provide up-to-date information on issues, trends, programs, policies, best practices, and technology in mathematics education.

> **S—Support** and sustain improved student achievement through the development of leadership skills and relationships among current and future mathematics leaders.

> **M—Motivate** mathematics leaders to maintain a lifelong commitment to provide equity and access for all learners.

As NCSM enters its fifth decade, we continue to strive for excellence and equity for all students. Our greatest challenge is developing the leadership knowledge and skills that will advance these central vision points. NCSM's future success depends on the extent to which mathematics education leaders can fulfill the vision and ideals outlined in *It's TIME*. Can we *network* with other stakeholders to ensure the next generation of mathematics education leaders are being prepared now? Can we *communicate* with and learn from one another the research regarding best-practice curriculum, instruction, and assessment? Can we passionately *support* improved student achievement initiatives? Can we seek to eradicate the social injustices that prevail in our schools and *motivate* equity and access goals for all learners? Yes, we can, and we will, because we are NCSM.

—The NCSM Board (2012–2013 and 2013–2014)

Introduction

■ ■ ■ ■

As an organization and as a profession, we unabatedly continue our fundamental goal of raising achievement in mathematics for *every* student. The Common Core State Standards for mathematics (CCSSM) provides clear guidance and poses new challenges that require a renewed commitment on the part of teachers, educational leaders, and policymakers to finally achieve this goal. As noted so compellingly in the CCSSM, these "standards are not just promises to our children, *but promises we intend to keep*" (National Governors Association Center for Best Practices & Council of Chief State School Officers [NGA & CCSSO], 2010, p. 5; emphasis added).

There is no way to ignore the fact that, since the 1990s, mathematics education reform has produced only marginal improvement and left many educators either searching for new and more productive solutions or unconvinced that the system is even capable of change. Too often we have tweaked the system at the margins and ignored critical alignments among components of the system. We have made a lot of promises but have not yet found ways to keep them. As leaders in mathematics education who acknowledge the limits of our individual and collective success, we believe we are in the best position to articulate a set of leadership imperatives and present a systemic framework to convert our shared vision into a reality of consistently high levels of mathematics learning for all students.

Given this context, *It's TIME* provides clear, research-based guidance on how to raise achievement in mathematics for *every* student and effectively implement the CCSSM in *every* classroom. That is, our purpose is to explicate a framework with a set of interrelated imperatives that constitute a call to action for systemic change in curriculum, instruction, assessment, and professional culture that is aligned with and supports the implementation of the CCSSM.

More specifically, this leadership framework for Common Core mathematics provides direction, justifications, suggestions, and resources for ensuring that all teachers of mathematics:

- Understand the mathematics that their students are expected to learn

- Possess the pedagogical content knowledge necessary to raise achievement

- Understand how the mathematics they teach is best sequenced and fits into curricular progressions across grades

- Envision and implement classrooms in which students are effectively engaged in learning mathematics and understand the instructional decisions that they need to make in order to create this environment

- Consistently implement high-quality instructional and formative assessment practices

- Have access to, and effectively use, high-quality instructional materials and resources

- Gather evidence of learning and make effective use of these data

- Create safe and supportive learning environments for all students

- Anticipate and plan for the needs of struggling students and respond with intensified learning experiences

- Practice their craft with specific and supportive feedback

- Engage in diverse opportunities for ongoing professional learning

- Collaborate with colleagues in a culture of trust and transparency

- Have the opportunity to be effectively coached

Additionally, this book provides guidance, justifications, and suggestions for ensuring that the educational system at the national, state, provincial, district, and school levels:

- Develops and disseminates a research-affirmed vision of effective teaching

- Addresses the beliefs and mindsets that often undermine change and improvement

- Designates and deploys a cadre of effectively trained mathematics program leaders

We argue that the outcome of these efforts should be a productive and shared culture of accountability, success and commitment to social justice, and celebration of accomplishments. We claim, based on our experiences and the research cited throughout this book, that when all of these elements are in place, we can expect an effective, consistent, and impactful implementation of the letter and spirit of the CCSSM and significantly higher levels of student achievement.

Figure I.1 displays our leadership framework. This framework summarizes the imperatives that constitute the call to action for successful implementation of the CCSSM and for high levels of performance on the Partnership for Assessment of Readiness for College and Careers (PARCC) and the Smarter Balanced Assessment Consortium (SBAC) assessments that are being designed to monitor growth in student achievement. Moreover, the framework, aligned with the contents of this book, takes the reader and leader from a set of givens, overarching themes, and supportive conditions to a set of imperatives that should result in a shared productive culture of accountability, commitment to success and social justice, and celebration of accomplishments. If the CCSSM represents clarity, coherence, and effectiveness of curriculum and instruction, *It's TIME* represents clarity, coherence, and effectiveness of the implementation of the CCSSM, with the dual goals of effective, consistent, and impactful implementation and significantly higher levels of student achievement in mathematics.

Specifically, we have identified a set of ten programmatic imperatives in the areas of knowledge, instruction and assessment, and systemic change

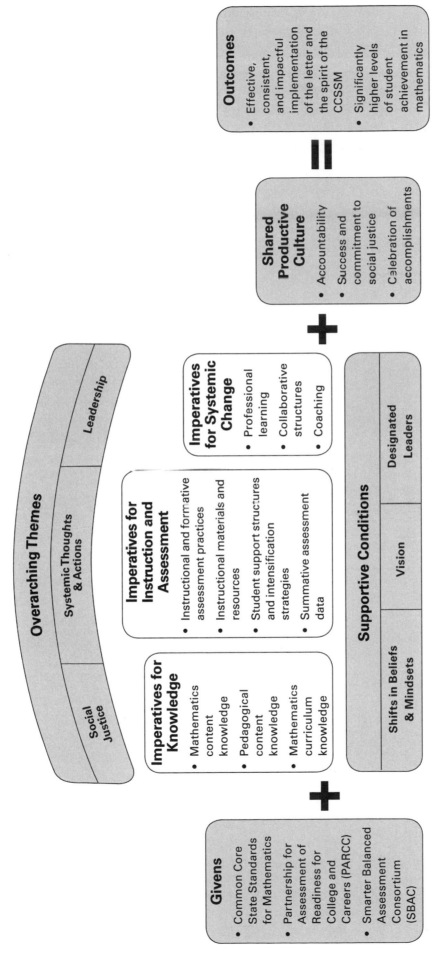

Figure I.1: Leadership framework for Common Core mathematics.

that leaders and teams of leaders are responsible for establishing to increase student learning.

Given both the breadth and the importance of this framework, *It's TIME* is intended for leaders, in the broadest sense, working together as leadership teams, responsible for moving or influencing individuals and groups toward a common goal of improving mathematics achievement for every student. Therefore, *leaders* include classroom teachers, mathematics specialists, and supervisors; mathematics coaches and department heads; supervisors, consultants, and mathematics resource personnel at the district, regional, state, and national levels; principals and instructional leaders; and university faculty.

At its core, this framework is a call to action to provide the focused leadership necessary to significantly improve the productivity of the mathematics education system. Our actions must impact every student in every classroom—no longer just reach some students in some classrooms. Our actions must build the capacity of both people and systems, not one to the exclusion of the other. Our actions must follow the guiding mantras that we're all in this together and together we can make a difference; we cannot tolerate the lack of opportunities for professional collaboration nor the professional isolation that limits growth. Our actions must recognize the systemic nature and interrelated components of the educational enterprise, meaning that tweaking at the margins and focusing on only one or two components will lead to failure. Finally, our actions must recognize that change of this magnitude takes time, is often uncomfortable, is rarely easy to accomplish, and cannot be done alone—but these cannot be excuses for delaying taking action. The time to begin is now!

Chapter 1
OVERARCHING THEMES

These are unique times in mathematics education. A high-quality set of common standards guide kindergarten through high school mathematics in most states, representing a long overdue, well-conceived internationally benchmarked curriculum. We have a much clearer sense of the instructional practices that raise achievement. Two state-led consortia, PARCC and SBAC, are developing technologically enhanced assessment systems explicitly aligned to the CCSSM. Teachers have unparalleled access to ideas and resources on the web that transfer to interactive whiteboards and other digital devices. Well-trained mathematics coaches are increasingly prevalent in schools. There is a much stronger research base to guide our actions than ever before. Thus, we have an emerging infrastructure that provides a stronger foundation for change and improvement than has previously existed.

But standards do not teach; teachers teach. It is the translation of standards into engaging tasks and powerful assessments in millions of classrooms that determines the quantity and quality of learning. It is *how* educators use available resources to provide an opportunity to learn that matters. Assessments are only valuable to the extent that the data are reliable and teachers use results to refine and improve instruction. Professional development that fails to provide opportunities for practice, feedback, and collaborative reflection has little real impact on teacher knowledge, teacher practice, or student achievement. All the research findings that fill our journals are of little use if they are not translated into practice. Most important of all, any honest interpretation of a broad array of National Assessment of Educational Progress (NAEP), Trends in International Mathematics and Science Study (TIMSS), and Programme for International Student Assessment (PISA) outcomes reveals that rarely does mathematics work for more than half of the student population, leaving an unacceptably high proportion of the population for whom the system has failed.

Before we can capitalize on the opportunities and address the challenges of the 21st century, we need to better understand why so little has changed. We have identified four factors to explain this lack of change and to frame the essential changes that need to be made.

1. There is a widespread lack of mathematics content knowledge and pedagogical content knowledge required for teachers to maximize student learning and to effectively implement the Common Core. This is not a statement of blame. Teachers and leaders were duly trained, certified, and hired. However, initial training and induction programs are often inadequate for first- and second-year teachers to be successful, certification requirements are frequently minimal, and opportunities for continued learning are very limited. Improvement and real change require a much more effective, ongoing system of developing mathematical and pedagogical content knowledge for all teachers of mathematics during every phase of their careers (Ma, 2010).

2. There are few mechanisms in place and insufficient time to improve mathematics content knowledge and pedagogical content knowledge. In too many schools and districts, teachers are poorly supervised, undersupported, and professionally isolated as they endure systems

of evaluation that too often are not aligned with research-affirmed instructional practices. Evaluation should be a process of continuous improvement, but in many places this is not the case. Improvement and real change require systematic, intensive, and high-quality coaching and dedicated allocations of time and structures for professional collaboration.

3. Too many schools fail to maximize the learning of their students. Again, this is not a statement of blame, but the facts are that few teachers have the benefit of a research-based vision of effective teaching practice. Far too many schools fail to make effective use of data to improve teaching and learning. In addition, teachers do not widely understand, encourage, model, or implement effective, high-leverage instructional practices in classrooms. The gap between what we know and what we do remains unacceptably wide. Improvement and real change require a much more effective system of supporting the teaching and learning process.

4. In mathematics education, to a much greater degree than in English language arts, our efforts are often severely stymied by a culture of beliefs and mindsets that lower expectations and limit the opportunity to learn. This is not to cast aspersions on people or systems, but we must acknowledge that mathematics is still frequently conceived as a sorter of talent and the rightful domain of only some. Many view mathematics as a nonessential domain of understanding and not as a critical source of empowerment for everyone. Too often, our perceptions, policies, and practices fail to provide opportunities for all students, and in far too many places, the link between high-quality mathematics education and social justice is missing from our actions, as students fall through cracks and leave school unprepared for the needs and expectations of today's workplace. Improvement and real change require reconceptualizing the unique role of mathematics in the development of an informed citizenry and a prepared workforce and having an unwavering commitment to the moral imperative to ensure mathematical proficiency for all.

Our challenge, and the purpose of this book, is to merge the unique opportunities we face with our understanding of the conditions that have compromised systemic change in the past to create an accessible and feasible framework for leaders and teams of leaders.

Before turning to the specific conditions and imperatives that leaders and teams of leaders must address to raise achievement in mathematics for *every* student and effectively implement the CCSSM in *every* classroom, we begin with three overarching themes for raising mathematics achievement: (1) social justice, (2) systemic thoughts and actions, and (3) leadership.

Social Justice

The CCSSM is composed of two significant dimensions. On one level, the CCSSM sets forth clear expectations for content understandings and

Three overarching themes for raising mathematics achievement:

1. Social justice

2. Systemic thoughts and actions

3. Leadership

standards for mathematical practice to ensure quality in what mathematics content is taught. On a second far more significant level, the CCSSM calls for social justice by demanding achievement in mathematics by *every* student. Effectively implementing the CCSSM requires schools to address both dimensions—high-quality content and a commitment to all students.

The direct link between mathematics education and social justice confronts us when Robert Moses and Charles Cobb declare algebra a civil right, when stark achievement gaps in mathematics among racial and ethnic groups remain the norm, and when policies and practices continue to systematically limit access to opportunities (Moses & Cobb, 2001). By *social justice*, we mean equality and fairness among diverse people. We advance social justice when we advocate for, expect, and achieve fair outcomes, basic rights, security, and opportunities in school and society. Equity in mathematics achievement refers to equitable *outcomes* for all students, not just equity of *access* or *opportunity*. In its position statement on equity in mathematics education, NCTM (2008) argues that "a culture of equity maximizes the learning potential of all students."

Conscious and unconscious biases—whether blatant, subtle, personal, or institutional—have inappropriately and unnecessarily compromised learning in school. These biases often lead to lower curricular and instructional expectations. When schools identify at-risk students based on "perceptions of student demographics and characteristics, such as past achievement, learning disability, language acquisition, ethnicity, learning style, family structure and family income" students' options can be limited (Stiff & Johnson, 2011, p. 86). When schools differentiate expectations for success, school experiences, and resources based on preconceived notions and bias, they cannot attain the goal of mathematical proficiency for all. Schools must identify and purge these biases.

In the broader sense, equipping all students with an awareness of the pressing political, health, environmental, economic, and social challenges—and a recognition of the critical role of mathematics in understanding and addressing these challenges—underscores mathematics as an engine of social justice by maximizing opportunity to participate fully in our society. Expecting, even demanding, that all students have the opportunity to engage in rigorous, relevant mathematics that is learned with high levels of cognitive demand also supports a social justice agenda. When all students have opportunities to become agents for change on these issues, we strengthen our society.

This is why an overarching prerequisite to strengthening mathematics programs is establishing safe and respectful school and classroom environments for students, teachers, other staff, and parents. Such environments have a culture of dignity for all, are free of harassment, and are welcoming to diverse backgrounds, beliefs, and ideas. These enabling environments send the message that all students are valued, can safely take risks, and know they belong.

Systemic Thoughts and Actions

Because our work in mathematics education revolves around a number of complex systems, we can only create lasting and productive change when we understand and account for the interconnected systems of our educational

---

"A culture of equity maximizes the learning potential of all students."

We can only create lasting and productive change when we understand and account for the interconnected systems of our educational enterprise.

enterprise. At its highest level, mathematics education operates within an interconnected system of students, teachers, and mathematics. We have the interrelated system of content (what teachers will teach), instruction (how teachers teach it), assessment (how well students learn it), and professional culture (how we interact and the beliefs we share). We have a systemic progression from teacher preparation to induction, to novice teaching, and to experienced practitioner. We have the interconnected knowledge of mathematics, specialized content knowledge for teaching mathematics, pedagogical knowledge, curriculum knowledge, and knowledge of students. And we have the critical support systems of time, resources, specialists, coaches, and leaders.

The surest way to limit one's impact is to attend to only one piece of a system, or to only one of these systems, without regard to how it affects the other pieces and systems. Efforts that merely tweak a single component seriously limit improvement and change. For example, adopting new instructional resources without commensurate professional development and coaching jeopardizes both the implementation of the materials and the relevance of the professional development. Similarly, focusing improvement only on enhancing mathematics content knowledge, without commensurate attention to pedagogical content knowledge required to make effective use of the mathematics content knowledge, also limits impact. When we ignore the need for coherence in our messages and alignment of our actions, we also seriously compromise impact. Thus, in *It's TIME*, while we categorize our imperatives into distinct components, schools must see and address them as but one element in an interconnected dynamic system. *It's TIME* will guide schools and leaders in linking all of their actions to the end goal of raising achievement in mathematics for *every* student and effectively implementing the CCSSM in *every* classroom.

Leadership

Finally, none of this is possible without guidance, nudging, cajoling, informing, and modeling—that is, leadership. It must be acknowledged that changing people's behavior is one of the most difficult aspects of leadership. There is, however, much that we know about changing behaviors.

- People cannot do what they cannot *envision*.

- People will not do what they do not *believe* is possible.

- People will not implement what they do not *understand*.

- People are unlikely to do well what they do not *practice*.

- People are unlikely to show much progress without *feedback*.

- People's efforts are unlikely to be sustained without *collaboration*.

The combination of these simple truisms leads us to the heart of providing effective leadership for school mathematics programs. Leaders at every level must help people envision, believe, understand, practice, receive feedback, and work collaboratively (Leinwand, 2012). That is, leaders and teams of leaders must be held, and must hold themselves, accountable for ensuring steady

None of this is possible without leadership.

progress toward the broad implementation of the leadership framework for Common Core mathematics.

Upon this foundation of overarching themes, we turn now to the supportive conditions that are essential prerequisites for systemic change.

Chapter 2
SUPPORTIVE CONDITIONS

Supportive conditions are the non-negotiable messages and program characteristics that ensure that teachers, leaders, and parents are all pulling in the same direction to see that every student can and will successfully learn mathematics. As such, supportive conditions undergird the specific actions teachers and leaders must take to facilitate success for every student. They serve as both a guide and a measure. More specifically, supportive conditions send a clear and consistent message of expectations and establish rules of acceptable conduct. The three supportive conditions we set forth for ensuring programmatic quality and coherence are (1) beliefs and mindsets that are based on research and not tied to preserving tradition and historical practice, (2) a shared vision, and (3) designated leaders. Without clarity about the beliefs and mindsets that support or undermine social justice and a commitment to quality, a program fails under the idiosyncrasies of individuals rather than succeeds due to the collective wisdom of the community. Without a vision, a program is rudderless. Without designated leaders, no one is positioned to assume responsibility for supporting and monitoring the overall success of the program.

Accordingly, to provide guidance, maintain perspective, and build capacity, the leaders and teams of leaders in every school and school district must:

- Address the beliefs and mindsets that guide action and determine willingness to change

- Develop and ensure widespread use of a written, shared vision of effective teaching and learning of mathematics

- Identify, designate, deploy, and support mathematics leaders at all necessary levels

Shifts in Beliefs and Mindsets

Teacher beliefs, the learning environment, and the school culture coalesce in the classroom teaching of mathematics (Guskey, 1986; Hoyles, 1992; Skott, 2001; Thompson, 1992). Few would argue against the assertion that every mathematics teacher wants his or her students to be successful and learn mathematics content. Research indicates that high-quality instruction leads to student achievement in mathematics, and individual and collective beliefs and mindsets are key determinants of instructional practices and classroom environments (Ash & D'Auria, 2013).

Mathematics teachers enter the profession with their own knowledge, attitudes, experiences, and beliefs about teaching, learning, and mathematics, each of which contributes to the manner in which teachers approach instruction and the type of learning environment they create. Accordingly, every school and district must attend to the diverse, and often competing, beliefs and mindsets about teaching and learning mathematics that permeate all aspects of K–12 mathematics programs.

For leaders in mathematics education, understanding the role that beliefs play in the work of teachers is crucial to providing targeted guidance and support for teachers of mathematics. Implementing the CCSSM, in particular the Standards for Mathematical Practice, requires that teachers have both the will and the capacity to facilitate instruction that enables

Leaders in every school and district must:

- *Address the beliefs and mindsets that guide action*

- *Develop a written, shared vision*

- *Designate mathematics leaders*

students to reason critically and make sense of the mathematics (NGA & CCSSO, 2010).

Mathematics teachers' beliefs can serve to advance or hinder the changes that the typical mathematics classroom requires as it implements the CCSSM. If a teacher believes students learn mathematics through an algorithmic approach of applying a set of procedures, he or she will struggle to teach mathematics as a sense-making activity (Battista, 1994). This teacher's approach to mathematics instruction will provide little or no opportunity for students to develop a conceptual understanding of the content. Nor will the teacher engage students in developing the processes and dispositions, including reasoning, justifying, generalizing, constructing viable arguments, and being precise, that are put forth in the Standards for Mathematical Practice in the CCSSM.

Teacher beliefs are also key factors in equity and social justice and the delivery of high-quality mathematics instruction to every student. The beliefs teachers have about students, society, and education can result in certain populations of students having limited access to the high level of rigor, depth of mathematics content, and breadth of practice (Sztajn, 2003) that are now exemplified by the Standards for Mathematical Practice and the CCSSM.

To make things easier for their students who may have challenges beyond the classroom, some teachers provide fewer opportunities for problem solving around rich mathematics, offer fewer chances to engage in meaningful discourse to reason about the content, and have lower expectations for the quality of work. While well intended, the beliefs and mindsets that undergird these actions have a direct impact on what students can learn and how, and that learning is limited.

A teacher's mindset can influence his or her approach to teaching mathematics. A teacher who believes intelligence is static has a fixed mindset (Dweck, 2006). In the eyes of this teacher, a student can either do mathematics or is not capable of learning high-level mathematics. Such a mindset becomes evident in the types of problems the teacher presents to students (such as skill based or algorithmic) and in the way the teacher communicates to students, for example, saying, "You are really smart if you can do this problem." On the other end of the spectrum is the teacher with a growth mindset (Dweck, 2006). A teacher with a growth mindset believes intelligence to be malleable and that, with effective effort, students can learn mathematics. This teacher is more likely to present students with appropriately challenging mathematics and provide the necessary supports to ensure learning of the content.

Although changing a teacher's beliefs or mindset can be challenging, Alba Thompson (1992) explains that "thoughtful analyses of the nature of the relationship between beliefs and practice suggest that belief systems are dynamic, permeable mental structures, susceptible to change in light of experience" (p. 140). Therein lies the challenge for leaders in mathematics education. Leaders must create the experiences and opportunities for reflection that cause teachers to examine their beliefs and how these beliefs align with the expectations of the CCSSM.

Linda Lambert (2002) asserts that when teachers' beliefs change, they view their instructional practice in new ways. She suggests that the work of leaders is to engage teachers in *sustained conversations* about teaching and learning mathematics. The leader is responsible for creating opportunities and conversations that challenge teacher beliefs. These conversations are part of the ongoing, regular dialogue between the leader and teacher, both informally and formally.

Ignoring the power of beliefs and mindsets or missing opportunities to shift beliefs and mindsets undermines the likelihood of change and improvement. Like nurturing a guiding vision, leaders and teams of leaders must attend to shifting beliefs and mindsets of all those who impact school mathematics programs.

Vision

A vision articulates our beliefs and values about conducting our work. A vision statement publically codifies these beliefs and values and makes them accessible to all stakeholders. More powerful than the generalities of typical philosophy statements and more specific than the broad platitudes of typical mission statements, effective vision statements delineate core behavioral expectations and program characteristics to best serve students.

In the absence of a shared vision, almost any practice is acceptable. Some teachers assign thirty homework problems each night, ignoring research on the importance of distributed practice (Rohrer, 2009) while other teachers limit homework to no more than ten problems with only a few that relate to what was taught that day; and the rest of the faculty provides opportunities for cumulative review and distributed practice. Some teachers make extensive use of practice worksheets and focus on using mathematics to get right answers, while other teachers strive to balance skills and concepts and actively engage students in thinking and reasoning about what they are learning. A common vision can help narrow these unacceptable variances and provide clear direction to coaches, supervisors, and administrators on how to guide teachers toward more consistent, more coherent, and more effective practice that balances skills and concepts and actively engages students in thinking and reasoning about what they are learning. Moreover, a vision statement that describes effective planning, high-leverage practices, and the expectation for reflection helps to create norms of behavior that support collaborative interaction.

Many states and districts talk about a shared vision of teaching and learning, but few explicitly describe the characteristics of a standards-based classroom. Massachusetts is a notable exception. The Massachusetts Department of Elementary and Secondary Education's (2009) document "Characteristics of a Standards-Based Mathematics Classroom" (see appendix A, page 61) describes effective classroom practice. It contains twenty characteristics and descriptive indicators in eight domains of practice, including learning standards, lesson organization, classroom environment, student learning, teaching, assessment, technology, and equity. The Massachusetts Department of Elementary and Secondary Education (2009) states, "Standards-based mathematics teaching and learning is a cooperative effort by teachers and students to actively engage in purposeful learning experiences that stimulate curiosity, enjoyment, and deep understanding of the mathematical concepts outlined in the Massachusetts Mathematics Curriculum Framework" (p. 1). In addition to presenting a statewide vision of effective mathematics classrooms, these characteristics and indicators are a resource for district and state professional development, instructional coaching, supervision of instruction, and classroom, school, and district accountability. More significantly, although district mathematics leaders developed the vision collaboratively, its existence and dissemination appear to represent a rare and powerful contribution on the part of the state into the realm of instructional practices.

A second example, developed by the Jefferson County Teachers Association (of Louisville, Kentucky), is the document "A Shared Vision of Effective Teaching and Learning of K–8 Mathematics in the Jefferson County Public Schools" (2007). See appendix B (page 71) for the full text of this document. This document provides an example-laden description of the key practices aligned with higher levels of student performance including effective planning, the use of alternative approaches, multiple representations and contexts, and providing cumulative review.

Key, but too often missing, first steps toward significant improvement are the collaborative crafting, widespread dissemination, and consistent referencing of a shared vision of effective mathematics teaching and learning evident in these two examples. Leaders and teams of leaders must ask themselves where this vision is in their schools and districts and, if necessary, assemble a team of educators to adapt, craft, or adopt a district-level statement of a shared vision of effective teaching of mathematics.

Designated Leaders

Leadership is not just a component of effectiveness and impact; it is also the designation of people who are explicitly assigned responsibility for planning, guiding, implementing, monitoring, and evaluating the activities and initiatives to support improvement. Designated leaders of mathematics programs provide direction and coordination in the areas of curriculum design, instructional resources, instructional practices, assessment, and professional development and ensure the alignment among these program components. They use a variety of strategies to communicate in writing and electronically with diverse stakeholders about the goals and objectives of the program. They forge partnerships to support the vision and goals of the program, and they provide a critical sense of urgency and high expectations for accomplishment that pervade the system. Without effective leadership, little change or improvement is likely.

If the primary role of classroom teachers is to *teach*, who provides guidance on *what* to teach, support for improving *how* to teach, assistance with interpreting assessment results, the link between communicating the needs of teachers and the expectations of administrators, and representation of the program's successes and needs to the broader community? The answer is *leaders*. These critical supportive roles require designated, trained, and empowered leaders who are responsible for coordinating the planning, implementation, and evaluation of all aspects of the mathematics program.

Responsibilities

As NCSM (2008) has noted, leaders are called on

> not to settle for the current state of "is-ness" in mathematics education, but rather to lead the pursuit of a better future for every child. Student achievement in mathematics is unlikely to improve significantly beyond current local, regional, state, national, or provincial levels until mathematics education leaders assume and exercise professional responsibility and accountability for their own practice and the practice of the teachers they lead. Leadership matters. A single mathematics education leader can have an incredible impact on the development and effectiveness of others. (p. 1)

Designated leaders, whether department heads, lead teachers, mathematics specialists, mathematics coaches, or mathematics supervisors, serve as informed resources, critical friends, and responsible managers for ensuring that everything required to support the work of teachers is in place and of value.

The following are responsibilities that school- and district-level mathematics program leaders should carry out in regard to curriculum design, instructional strategies and materials, assessment, professional development, and partnerships (NCSM, 1998).

To support curriculum design, leaders should:

- Coordinate the development and implementation of a sound and coherent K–12 mathematics curriculum

- Ensure curricular alignment and coordination between grades, levels, and courses, including helping teachers understand the curriculum as a whole and their part in it

- Assist teachers in using rich and challenging problems and activities that integrate mathematics into other disciplines and the content of other disciplines into mathematics

- Guide the ongoing review and revision of the curriculum and ensure alignment with state and local guidelines

To support instructional strategies and materials, leaders should:

- Recommend programs and materials and oversee their piloting, adoption, and evaluation

- Consult with and acquaint teachers with successful and innovative strategies, including translating research findings into practice

- Assist teachers in effectively using technology in daily instruction

- Model effective instructional strategies for teachers

- Work with teachers to encourage reflection and discussion of what is working, what is not working, and how to make improvements

To support assessment, leaders should:

- Assist teachers in designing and implementing a broad range of assessment tools

- Ensure the alignment of assessment instruments with the curriculum

- Collect and analyze data about what is and is not working and use the data, including student assessment results, to improve curriculum and instruction

- Interpret the results of assessments for parents and the community at large

To support professional development, leaders should:

- Collaborate with the staff to determine needs and priorities for professional development

- Conduct or facilitate professional development activities and motivate colleagues to engage in ongoing professional growth and development

- Encourage and facilitate ongoing professional collaboration and effective collaborative structures

- Encourage involvement in professional organizations

- Promote the mentoring of colleagues and professional visits among teachers

To support partnerships, leaders should:

- Communicate with committees, school boards, administrators, teachers, parents, and students about the importance of mathematics and the need for high-quality mathematics programs

- Cultivate connections with the postsecondary mathematics and mathematics education communities and with local business and industry personnel

- Establish and support forums and encourage dialogue among groups that influence the shape and direction of school mathematics programs

It is impossible to envision a pathway to raising achievement in mathematics for *every* student and effectively implement the CCSSM in *every* classroom without attention to beliefs and mindsets, a shared vision, and the designation of mathematics program leaders. These three supportive conditions constitute the foundation for improvement that effective leaders create.

Chapter 3

IMPERATIVES FOR KNOWLEDGE

When mathematics teachers have high levels of requisite knowledge, use research-based high-leverage instructional practices and resources, and use evidence of learning to plan and implement daily instruction in meaningful ways, they maximize students' learning. This chapter describes the necessary three program components centered around teachers' requisite knowledge: (1) mathematics content knowledge, (2) pedagogical content knowledge, and (3) mathematics curriculum knowledge. We identify the critical elements of these imperatives and link them directly to the end goal of raising achievement in mathematics for *every* student and effectively implementing the CCSSM in *every* classroom.

Mathematics Content Knowledge

Raising achievement in mathematics for *every* student and effectively implementing the CCSSM in *every* classroom requires that *teachers understand the mathematics content that they expect students to learn.* Mathematics content knowledge refers to a person's understanding of the skills, concepts, applications, reasoning methods, and connections within mathematics that are prerequisite to what is being taught, are aligned with what is being taught, and build from what is being taught.

To ensure that teachers understand the mathematics content that students are expected to learn, leaders and teams of leaders must:

- Establish an understanding of the scope of mathematics content knowledge

- Support an understanding of the breadth and depth of mathematics content knowledge

- Create opportunities for teachers to identify deficiencies and develop mathematical content knowledge to fill the gaps

Establish an Understanding of the Scope of Mathematics Content Knowledge

As stated in *Principles and Standards for School Mathematics* (NCTM, 2000), "Teachers need to understand the big ideas of mathematics and be able to represent mathematics as a coherent and connected enterprise" (p. 17). By *big ideas* we mean those ideas that are, as Randall Charles (2005) explains, "central to the learning of mathematics and that link numerous mathematical understandings into a coherent whole" (p. 10). Big ideas are not simply topics, strands, or objectives. Mathematics is much more than a list of topics; it is the study of quantity, change, chance, shape, and dimension, which is comprised of big ideas like place value, equivalence, function, and iteration.

Support an Understanding of the Breadth and Depth of Mathematics Content Knowledge

Mathematics represents an interrelated set of skills and concepts that go far beyond merely learning rules to get correct answers. The mathematics content knowledge that is required of teachers must balance how to use mathematics

*Raising achievement in mathematics for **every** student and effectively implementing the CCSSM in **every** classroom requires that **teachers understand the mathematics content that they expect students to learn.***

with why the mathematics works. If mathematics is to make sense to students, it must make sense to their teachers. *Adding It Up* (Kilpatrick, Swafford, & Findell, 2001) posits that mathematical proficiency has five strands.

1. Conceptual understanding: Comprehension of mathematical concepts, operations, and relations

2. Procedural fluency: Skill in carrying out procedures flexibly, accurately, efficiently, and appropriately

3. Strategic competence: Ability to formulate, represent, and solve mathematical problems

4. Adaptive reasoning: Capacity for logical thought, reflection, explanation, and justification

5. Productive disposition: Habitual inclination to see mathematics as sensible, useful, and worthwhile, coupled with a belief in diligence and one's own efficacy

Students can only develop this proficiency if their teachers bring it into the classroom. The CCSSM promotes teaching fewer concepts, but teaching them in more depth, with deeper understanding as the goal. However, teachers must have a deep understanding of the content themselves to teach for deeper understanding.

Mathematics involves more than just recalling facts and performing routine procedures. Mathematics needs to be understood as an integrated collection of knowledge and skills, not as a series of discrete procedures. Mathematics must also be understood as connected to other disciplines and to the world in which we live. A technology- and information-based society requires citizens to be able to think, reason, and analyze. Knowing mathematics means being able to adapt and apply mathematical ideas to new situations and to a variety of problems.

Create Opportunities for Teachers to Identify Deficiencies and Develop Mathematics Content Knowledge

Too often, professional development focuses only on pedagogy or activities that are unrelated to content. More professional development needs to focus on content and the development of student understanding. Furthermore, leaders must work with teachers to help them analyze the content they are teaching and to determine if there is content that they do not fully understand. This requires a supportive environment where teachers feel comfortable admitting what they do not understand. This could be accomplished by grade-level and cross-grade-level collaboration, book studies, presentations on specific mathematical content, and professional development opportunities. Teachers need to realize their own knowledge gaps and be willing to ask for help. Teachers should have access to a coach or mathematics specialist to whom they can address questions about content and to a range of instructional resources that provide guidance on the mathematical ideas

To ensure that teachers understand the mathematics content that students are expected to learn:

- *Establish an understanding of the scope of mathematics content knowledge*

- *Support an understanding of the breadth and depth of mathematics content knowledge*

- *Create opportunities for teachers to identify deficiencies and develop mathematical content knowledge* needed for teaching. These resources could include university mathematics content and methods manuals and textbooks, *The Common Core State Standards for Mathematics*, and books such as the National Council of Teachers of Mathematics's *The Developing Essential Understanding Series*. For additional suggestions, please see the section on instructional materials and resources in chapter 4. Professional development opportunities should include, but not be limited to, grade-level and cross-grade-level discussions of the specific content and university courses that focus on mathematics content.

It will be evident that content knowledge is increasing when:

- Teachers consistently demonstrate an understanding of mathematics that transcends using rules to get correct answers

- Classroom observations consistently reveal accurate, appropriate, and effective presentation and explanation of the mathematics being taught

- Classroom observations consistently reveal carefully crafted series of questions that elicit and illuminate the mathematics being taught

- Teachers report a range of available opportunities to learn the mathematics content their students are expected to learn

Pedagogical Content Knowledge

Raising achievement in mathematics for *every* student and effectively implementing the CCSSM in *every* classroom requires that *teachers understand what teaching approaches best fit the content and how to best organize the elements of the content for effective teaching*. Pedagogical content knowledge is the critical knowledge that links specific mathematics content with effective mathematics instruction. It represents a blend of what content to teach and how best to teach it. More specifically, pedagogical content knowledge includes the following.

- Planning: Identifying problems and tasks that match skills or expectations and the key mathematical understandings that result from any given problem or task

- Teaching: Identifying appropriate explanations, questions, models, approaches, and next steps

- Assessing: Understanding student reasoning and effectively dealing with common errors and misconceptions

To ensure effective teaching that incorporates these functions, leaders and teams of leaders should:

- Establish an understanding that content and pedagogy are inseparable components of effective teaching and that mathematics content knowledge is necessary but not sufficient for effectively teaching mathematics

- Support the understanding that there is a body of pedagogical content knowledge for effective instruction that informs the selection

*Raising achievement in mathematics for **every** student and effectively implementing the CCSSM in **every** classroom requires that **teachers understand what teaching approaches best fit the content and how to best organize the elements of the content for effective teaching**.*

of tasks and activities; guides appropriate approaches, models, explanations, and questions; and addresses common errors and misconceptions

- Help educators identify individual and collective pedagogical content knowledge gaps and deficiencies, and then provide diverse opportunities for teachers to learn the necessary pedagogical content knowledge for effective instruction

Establish an Understanding That Content and Pedagogy Are Inseparable Components of Effective Teaching

With pedagogical content knowledge, teachers understand how to *support* students' mathematics learning so that they can solve problems and understand the fundamental ideas. Teachers having this content knowledge will make the difference between merely teaching by telling *how* and teaching by understanding *why*. Leaders must be held accountable for ensuring that teachers have the content knowledge and the instructional skills to help students increase their mathematical understanding. Leaders must be able to model appropriate instruction, find resources, ask deep questions to ensure understanding, and guide teachers to improve their mathematics knowledge and repertoire of instructional strategies.

Support the Understanding That There Is a Body of Pedagogical Content Knowledge for Effective Instruction

Through planning, pedagogical content knowledge involves selecting appropriate tasks and activities to support the student learning of specific mathematical skills or ideas. Tasks must be appropriate for the content knowledge intended and for the extensions necessary to allow students to think critically, solve problems, and communicate mathematics.

Pedagogical content knowledge includes an understanding of what makes concepts easy or difficult to learn and which models or representations work best for individual students. For example, it is the understanding and appropriate use of a repertoire of representations from symbols to number lines to concrete models to area models that support the effective teaching of a topic like multiplication of fractions. When a grade 6 Common Core standard states, "Use ratio and rate reasoning to solve real-world and mathematical problems, e.g., by reasoning about tables of equivalent ratios, tape diagrams, double number line diagrams, or equations" (6.RP.A.3; NGA & CCSSO, 2010, p. 42), teachers need pedagogical content knowledge to decide how, when, and with whom to deploy these different representations.

Pedagogical content knowledge also comes into play when teachers address common mistakes and misconceptions. For example, when learning about complementary and supplementary angles, a student responds that the supplement of 63° is 27°, rather than 117°; or when reasoning about shapes, a student responds that all rectangles are squares, rather than all squares are rectangles. In both cases, it is a teacher's pedagogical content knowledge

To ensure effective teaching that incorporates these functions:

- *Establish an understanding that content and pedagogy are inseparable*

- *Support the understanding that there is a body of pedagogical content knowledge for effective instruction*

- *Help educators identify pedagogical content knowledge deficiencies, and provide opportunities for teachers to learn the necessary knowledge* that comes into play when helping these students resolve their mistakes and misconceptions.

Help Educators Identify Pedagogical Content Knowledge Gaps, and Provide Opportunities for Them to Learn

While we can learn mathematics content knowledge in college courses and traditional professional development settings, to learn pedagogical content knowledge, teachers need students and classrooms. It is unreasonable to expect new teachers to possess this knowledge; therefore, it is essential to build structures and opportunities to develop this knowledge in job-embedded professional growth models like lesson studies, classroom observations, video analyses, and reviews of student work. Many teachers also attend grant-funded or school-district-sponsored workshops, institutes, or seminars to advance their content and pedagogical knowledge. The collaborative structures discussed in chapter 5 are key components of building this pedagogical content knowledge.

It will be evident that teachers are building pedagogical content knowledge when:

- They consistently demonstrate that content and pedagogy are inseparable components of effective teaching by teaching through project-based learning, problem applications, and within new situations

- Classroom observations consistently reveal effective and appropriate selection of tasks and activities; approaches, models, explanations, and questions for conveying mathematics; and effective responses to common errors and misconceptions by students

- They report a range of opportunities are available to learn the pedagogical content knowledge they need

Mathematics Curriculum Knowledge

Raising achievement in mathematics for *every* student and effectively implementing the CCSSM in *every* classroom requires that *teachers understand how to best sequence, connect, and situate the content they are expected to teach within learning progressions.* Mathematics curriculum knowledge is an understanding of how to sequence and organize the content for teaching. Teachers understand how best to sequence mathematics content in coherent learning progressions within and across grades and courses, what the big ideas of mathematics are, and how mathematical ideas are connected with other disciplines.

To deliver an effective mathematics curriculum, leaders and teams of leaders must:

- Ensure teachers understand how and why focus, depth, and coherence make a mathematics curriculum effective

- Develop and deepen understandings of learning progressions of key mathematical topics within a grade and across grades

*Raising achievement in mathematics for **every** student and effectively implementing the CCSSM in **every** classroom requires that **teachers understand how to best sequence, connect, and situate the content they are expected to teach within learning progressions.***

- Organize the CCSSM content expectations for each grade or course into feasible teaching guides that link content standards, big ideas, and instructional resources

- Create opportunities for teachers to investigate the curriculum at their grade level and across grade levels to fully understand the curriculum they expect students to learn

Ensure Teachers Understand How and Why Focus, Depth, and Coherence Make a Mathematics Curriculum Effective

Traditionally, the U.S. curriculum has been referred to as being a "mile wide and an inch deep." The Center for the Study of Mathematics Curriculum reaffirms how overcrowded most state mathematics curriculum standards have become (Reys, Dingman, Sutter, & Teuscher, 2005). A crowded curriculum is not a focused curriculum. Rather than racing to cover everything, teachers must narrow and deepen the content. The CCSSM has fewer concepts at each grade or course level, which teachers can teach thoroughly. By focusing intensely on the major concepts, students gain a stronger foundation in conceptual understanding, achieve fluency with skills, and apply the mathematics to other situations. Additionally, the curriculum should be coherent to support teaching and learning. Schmidt, Wang, and McKnight (2005) argue that standards are coherent if they specify topics, including the depth at which the topic is to be studied, as well as sequence the topics, both within and across each grade. The curriculum used at a school and within a district should be based on standards that are coherent.

Develop and Deepen Understandings of Learning Progressions

A coherent curriculum must carefully connect learning within and across grades so students bridge knowledge from previous years to new understanding. Underlying the CCSSM is a series of progressions or trajectories. Trajectories are hypotheses about the levels or steps that students are likely to go through as they learn mathematics. Learning takes place over time, and instruction needs to focus on what students already know and what learning comes next. Standards are not disconnected topics but are extensions of previous learning. Teachers understand the grade-level mathematics they are teaching but often do not know the mathematics that their students should have learned previously. Vertical team discussions of the mathematics content are imperative so that teachers understand the full scope of the mathematics that is taught before and after the grade they teach. Many lack understanding of how the particular concepts they are teaching relate to the mathematics that will follow in higher grades or other courses. Often, teachers introduce mathematics topics before establishing prerequisite knowledge. To help teachers gain this broad picture of mathematics, they must collaborate with mathematics teachers at other grade levels. The curriculum must have the content sequenced in such a way that each concept is built on previously developed concepts.

To deliver an effective mathematics curriculum:

- *Ensure teachers understand how and why focus, depth, and coherence make a mathematics curriculum effective*

- *Develop and deepen understandings of learning progressions*

- *Organize the CCSSM content expectations for each grade or course into feasible teaching guides*

- *Create opportunities for teachers to investigate the curriculum at their grade level and across grade levels*

Vertical team discussions of the mathematics content are imperative so that teachers understand the full scope of the mathematics that is taught before and after the grade they teach.

Organize the Content Expectations for Each Grade or Course Into Feasible Teaching Guides

The CCSSM provides a starting point with which to establish a local curriculum, but leaders must work collaboratively with teachers to develop teaching guides based on these standards. These guides must show connections among lessons, grade levels, and courses, thus allowing students to develop concepts in more depth. NCSM's (2008) *The PRIME Leadership Framework* states that the curriculum should include directions for introducing, extending, and formalizing content from previous grades, with emphasis on the connections among related topics. The guides must be based on the big ideas referenced in the mathematics content knowledge section of this chapter (page 20), link content standards, and include references to instructional resources that will help teachers implement the content standards. Leaders should provide teachers with a pacing guide to help them accomplish their goals. The CCSSM has changed the grade-level placement of many concepts. The teaching guides that leaders and teachers create in schools should explicitly identify what content the standards have changed per each grade level. For example, in the area of fractions, a much heavier emphasis is placed in grades 3–5 than was found in traditional curricula. Fluency of the standard algorithm for addition and subtraction of multi-digit numbers is now found in fourth grade, where before it might have been found in second grade.

Create Opportunities for Teachers to Develop Mathematics Curriculum Knowledge

Traditionally, teachers considered the textbook to be the curriculum, which they supplemented with an array of resource materials. Many teachers did not question the concepts or how they presented them; they simply followed the textbook. Teachers must become more involved in determining the curriculum. They need to be provided time to study the curriculum in small groups, with discussions centering around clarification of vocabulary, content, focus, coherency, and ways to go into greater depth in a lesson.

It will be evident that teachers are developing mathematics curriculum knowledge when:

- They consistently plan and implement lessons and units that reflect a coherent focus on important mathematical ideas

- Classroom observations consistently reveal accurate, appropriate, and effective sequencing of the mathematics being taught

- They make consistent and effective use of regularly updated grade-level or course teaching guides

- They report a range of available opportunities to develop an understanding of the mathematics curriculum knowledge that relates to what their students are expected to learn

Visit **go.solution-tree.com/mathematics** for links to relevant online resources related to the topics discussed in this chapter.

Chapter 4

IMPERATIVES FOR INSTRUCTION AND ASSESSMENT

In this chapter, we identify four imperatives that are essential for effective instruction and productive assessment to maximize learning for all students: (1) consistent implementation of research-affirmed instructional and formative assessment practices, (2) use of high-quality instructional materials and resources aligned with the CCSSM content, (3) availability of intensification strategies to support struggling students, and (4) summative assessment data that guide instructional planning.

Instructional and Formative Assessment Practices

Raising achievement in mathematics for *every* student and effectively implementing the CCSSM in *every* classroom requires that teachers consistently implement *effective, research-affirmed instructional and formative assessment practices in every classroom*. Instructional practices pertain to actions teachers or teacher teams take to plan lessons, make decisions, and analyze and reflect on student learning. These practices include selecting and sequencing appropriate problems, tasks, activities, and questions while employing diverse approaches and representations. Teachers use formative assessment practices during lesson planning and implementation to gather evidence about student learning and adjust instruction to better meet student needs. If teachers do not use the information to adjust instruction, it is not *formative*.

To ensure that teachers consistently implement effective, research-affirmed instructional and formative assessment practices in every classroom, leaders and teams of leaders must:

- Provide opportunities for teachers to plan and prepare together

- Provide opportunities for all educators to envision and implement high-quality instructional practices

- Monitor and provide feedback regarding student engagement and learning

- Engage teachers in reflection about instruction and learning

Provide Opportunities for Teachers to Plan and Prepare Together

Planning should not be done in isolation. To build effective instructional practices, leaders need to provide opportunities for teachers to collaborate to design instruction and reflect on individual practice (NCSM, 2007; NCSM, 2008; Kanold, 2012a, 2012b). The lesson-planning tool on page 74 in appendix C can be used to facilitate this process.

Because the CCSSM is based on learning progressions, teachers should spend a significant amount of time discussing the content and defining the depth of each standard and cluster before entering the classroom and studying how topics are developed across grade levels before a lesson begins. However, planning does not end with an understanding of the content. Teachers must understand how to implement learning activities and mathematical tasks that are engaging and challenging for students. To do this, teachers must learn about their students' interests, social and cultural characteristics, and background knowledge (Danielson, 2007, 2011; Martin, 2007).

Understanding and analyzing students' mathematical thinking is very important and requires careful planning. *Mathematics Teaching Today* (Martin, 2007) identifies ways in which teachers should attend to students' thinking in their planning and teaching, including:

- Understanding the mathematical concepts that teachers will develop during the lesson

- Anticipating the variety of strategies students may use in solving a problem as well as the misconceptions or difficulties they may have

- Asking questions to elicit students' thinking and advance understanding

Provide Opportunities for All Educators to Envision and Implement High-Quality Instructional Practices

In 1995, the Third International Mathematics and Science Study (TIMSS) found that in typical U.S. mathematics classrooms, teachers spent a considerable amount of time checking homework, demonstrating procedures, asking questions about process, and allowing time for independent practice (Lynch School of Education, n.d.). The fifth TIMSS administration in 2011 (now known as the Trends in International Mathematics and Science Study) confirmed the same findings (National Center for Education Statistics, n.d.). The researchers also found that teachers often presented definitions and required students to memorize them. The majority of problems teachers assigned focused on practicing the use of a single, previously taught procedure. This description of typical practice differs greatly from the classroom that adopts the eight Standards for Mathematical Practice (NGA & CCSSO, 2010), which include:

1. Making sense of problems and persevering in solving them

2. Reasoning abstractly and quantitatively

3. Constructing viable arguments and critiquing the reasoning of others

4. Modeling with mathematics

5. Using appropriate tools strategically

6. Attending to precision

7. Looking for and making use of structure

8. Looking for and expressing regularity in repeated reasoning

It is critical that teachers possess knowledge and understanding that support these practices as well as the ability necessary to first envision them and then translate them into actions.

Most teachers learned mathematics in classrooms that focused on mathematical facts and procedures. The overarching goal was to ensure

To ensure that teachers consistently implement effective, research-affirmed instructional and formative assessment practices in every classroom:

- *Provide opportunities for teachers to plan and prepare together*

- *Provide opportunities for all educators to envision and implement high-quality instructional practices*

- *Monitor and provide feedback regarding student engagement and learning*

- *Engage teachers in reflection about instruction and student learning*

that students could quickly and accurately get right answers. When the vision of mathematics expands to include mathematical reasoning, problem solving, communication, and representation, teachers need guidance and opportunities to envision different instructional practices. Mathematics leaders support this vision by providing teams with opportunities for reflection through the use of lesson studies and instructional rounds or through any intentional observations of their colleagues. Following are nine research-affirmed instructional practices that correlate with high levels of student achievement to incorporate into all mathematics instruction at all levels (Leinwand, n.d.).

1. Effective teachers of mathematics respond to most student answers with "why?," "how do you know that?," or "can you explain your thinking?"

2. Effective teachers of mathematics conduct daily cumulative review of critical and prerequisite skills and concepts at the beginning of every lesson.

3. Effective teachers of mathematics elicit, value, and celebrate alternative approaches to solving mathematics problems so that students are taught that mathematics is a sense-making process for understanding why and not memorizing the right procedure to get the one right answer.

4. Effective teachers of mathematics provide multiple representations—for example, models, diagrams, number lines, tables and graphs, as well as symbols—of all mathematical work to support the visualization of skills and concepts.

5. Effective teachers of mathematics create language-rich classrooms that emphasize terminology, vocabulary, explanations and solutions.

6. Effective teachers of mathematics take every opportunity to develop number sense by asking for, and justifying, estimates, mental calculations and equivalent forms of numbers.

7. Effective teachers of mathematics embed the mathematical content they are teaching in contexts to connect the mathematics to the real world.

8. Effective teachers of mathematics devote the last five minutes of every lesson to some form of formative assessments, for example, an exit slip, to assess the degree to which the lesson's objective was accomplished.

9. Effective teachers of mathematics demonstrate through the coherence of their instruction that their lessons—the tasks, the activities, the questions and the assessments—were carefully planned.

Characteristics of successful classrooms include using instructional groups, spending minimal time on noninstructional tasks, and having well-established rituals and routines (Danielson, 2011). Often, teachers tend to begin instruction without first establishing an environment that is conducive to learning. Danielson (2007) points out that students cannot concentrate on content until they feel comfortable in the classroom. A collaborative classroom that focuses on learning from mistakes is a great place to start. Wrong answers are as much a part of the process of understanding mathematics as correct answers. Thus, teachers must create a learning environment that is safe, where all ideas and methods are valued, students choose and share their methods, mistakes are learning sites for everyone, and correctness resides in mathematical argument (Martin, 2007).

Monitor and Provide Feedback Regarding Student Engagement and Learning

The process of implementing formative assessments begins with clearly identifying what students are expected to learn. Teachers embed formative assessment instruments and strategies into regular instruction. Formative assessments provide teachers and students with information about students' current thinking and misconceptions to enable better day-to-day instructional decision making and more meaningful student participation thus providing teachers a process to monitor and provide feedback to students as well as to adjust teaching strategies. Frequent and focused formative assessments produce significant, and often substantial, learning (Wiliam, 2011).

The following are assessment practices in classrooms and schools in which students perform at high levels.

- Teachers' use of formative assessments helps clearly identify the content that students are expected to know and be able to do. The content is clearly articulated to students, is appropriate to the grade level, and is delivered with sound instructional strategies.

- Teachers utilize a variety of assessment strategies that align with the content and embed them in daily instruction.

- Teachers understand that formative assessments are a continuous process of gathering information about student understanding of mathematics and making informed instructional decisions based on those understandings.

- Teachers use the assessment results to plan instruction for the class, groups, and individual students.

- Teachers reflect on assessment results and use the findings to identify any content for which they should seek professional development to enhance the content knowledge or to extend the pedagogy options to improve student understanding.

See the tool on page 76 in appendix C for five common approaches to conducting effective formative assessment.

*Raising achievement in mathematics for **every** student and effectively implementing the CCSSM in **every** classroom requires **instructional materials that align with the mathematics content and practices of the CCSS for mathematics, create excitement and motivation, and are developmentally appropriate. These materials must support the planning, implementation, and assessment of high-quality lessons***.

Engage Teachers in Reflection About Instruction and Learning

A true mark of professionalism is a teacher's ability to reflect on his or her teaching (Danielson, 2007). Effective teachers reflect on student learning and understanding and on their own teaching. A key function of the collaborative structures discussed in the following sections is to provide focused, collaborative opportunities to reflect on teaching and its impact.

It will be evident that teachers are reflecting on instruction and student learning when they are consistently:

- Choosing good problems—problems that invite exploration of an important mathematical concept and allow students the chance to solidify and extend their knowledge

- Assessing students' understanding by listening to discussions and asking students to justify their responses

- Using questioning techniques to facilitate students' learning and reasoning

- Encouraging students to explore multiple solutions

- Challenging students to think more deeply about the problems they are solving and to make connections to other ideas within mathematics

- Using multiple representations to foster a variety of mathematical perspectives

- Creating a variety of opportunities, such as group work and class discussions, for students to communicate mathematically

- Modeling appropriate mathematical language and strategies, with a disposition for solving challenging mathematical problems

- Targeting instruction based on students' needs and providing additional support

It will be evident that teachers are reflecting on instruction and student learning when students are consistently (Martin, 2007):

- Engaging actively in the learning process

- Using existing mathematical knowledge to make sense of assigned tasks

- Making connections among mathematical concepts

- Reasoning and making conjectures about a problem

- Communicating their mathematical thinking orally and in writing

- Listening and reacting to others' thinking and solutions to problems

- Using a variety of representations, such as pictures, tables, graphs, and words, for their mathematical thinking

- Using mathematical and technological tools, such as physical materials, calculators, and computers, along with textbooks and other instructional resources

- Building new mathematical knowledge through problem solving and understanding

Instructional Materials and Resources

Raising achievement in mathematics for *every* student and effectively implementing the CCSSM in *every* classroom requires *instructional materials that align with the mathematics content and practices of the CCSS for mathematics, create excitement and motivation, and are developmentally appropriate. These materials must support the planning, implementation, and assessment of high-quality lessons.* Instructional materials and resources are any concrete objects, digital devices, digital and print media, and support materials for lesson planning that enhance the teaching and learning process.

To ensure that instructional materials create excitement and motivation, are developmentally appropriate, and support the planning, implementation, and assessment of high-quality lessons, leaders and teams of leaders must:

- Provide access to rich instructional resources

- Guide the selection of instructional resources to create a research-affirmed best practice mathematics learning environment

- Involve teachers in the selection of instructional resources aligned with the CCSSM

Provide Access to Rich Instructional Resources

Leaders should have an effective plan for acquiring or providing access to a wide variety of instructional resources and tools for teaching and learning. It may be necessary for teams of leaders to provide support and funding so every teacher can acquire and use necessary tools to benefit all students of a grade level or course. An assortment of all kinds of tools should be readily available to students to support mathematical exploration that highlights the development of student understanding (Kanold, 2012b). These might include technology-based tools and nontechnology tools such as manipulatives, measuring devices, and hands-on materials. Teachers must give students support in selecting appropriate tools for particular mathematics tasks and help students with their understanding when some tools are a hindrance.

Textbooks tend to have a significant impact on what content teachers teach and how they present it (Reys & Bay-Williams, 2003). However, not all textbooks are alike. Good textbooks have the potential to promote quality instruction and the implementation of a comprehensive mathematics curriculum, but the textbook is *not* the curriculum. Accordingly, textbooks must be seen as tools to be used with care. When mathematics classrooms implement traditional textbooks, it is essential that teachers focus on the big ideas, conceptual understandings, and Standards for Mathematical Practice—instead of the pages in the textbook—to help implement high-quality instruction. Rather than marching lesson by lesson through a

To ensure that instructional materials create excitement and motivation, are developmentally appropriate, and support high-quality lessons:

- *Provide access to rich instructional resources*

- *Guide the selection of instructional resources*

- *Involve teachers in the selection of instructional resources*

textbook, teachers must select lessons that match the CCSSM, classroom instructional goals, and students' needs. Increasingly, such lessons are available on the Internet, but they need careful screening and review to ensure their appropriateness.

Guide the Selection of Instructional Resources

Teachers need guidance on how best to select and organize instructional resources. If the materials do not have the potential to reveal important mathematical ideas, then they may not be useful. The emphasis must be on student understanding of the mathematics, and the instructional resources need to be clearly linked to concept development. The process of selecting these instructional resources can lead to more effective teaching and learning practices (Loucks-Horsley, Love, Stiles, Mundry, & Hewson, 2003).

Manipulatives are tools that can engage students in exploring concepts and constructing their own meaning from concrete representations of mathematical ideas. For example, a variety of hands-on tools, used effectively, provides students the opportunity to create multiple representations, such as representing fractions with circular parts of a region, using a number line, and drawing a picture. Representing concepts in a variety of ways accommodates diverse learners. In addition, manipulatives have the potential to guide informal and formal classroom discussions that are integral in developing mathematics concepts. Increasingly, virtual manipulatives are an accessible and inexpensive addition to physical models.

Technology and digital resources, such as calculators, computers, online manipulatives, iPads and tablets, and whiteboards, are also essential tools for 21st century mathematics classrooms. Such resources are not luxury items. However, the key is *how* students experience these technologies and *how* classrooms use them to support the development of mathematical concepts. Technology-enhanced learning environments help students make real-life connections to mathematical concepts. These digital devices become tools for collaborative, creative learning to enhance engagement and motivation of students in mathematics classrooms.

To have proficient language skills, students will need to use mathematical vocabulary again and again in meaningful contexts until they internalize the words (Leinwand, 2009). Literature, stories, and poems create real-life purposes that illuminate mathematics content significance outside the mathematics classroom and help make mathematical learning personal and meaningful while enhancing mathematics concepts. Writing in the mathematics classroom is not just a method of communication and expression; improving writing skills improves one's capacity to learn (Goldsby & Cozza, 2002; Stonewater, 2002). A literacy-rich environment can provide a bridge to new terms and meanings to enable new information to be assimilated into students' existing schemata.

Involve Teachers in the Selection of Instructional Resources Aligned With the CCSSM

Leaders must ensure that teachers select instructional resources that align with the CCSSM. Mathematics leaders need to create structures to build capacity for defining high-quality instructional resources. Structures could include but are not limited to curriculum teams and professional development.

Involvement in these structures increases teachers' understanding of the relationship between the curriculum and the CCSSM and gives them insight into the intent of the CCSSM. Actively participating in pilot testing of instructional resources helps teachers see how the curriculum works with students and informs the professional development needed to support implementation (Loucks-Horsley et al., 2003). Once teachers make a variety of tools available to students, they should provide students with support in selecting appropriate tools for a particular mathematics task (Kanold, 2012a).

It will be evident that teachers are involved with selecting instructional resources and are committed to implementation with fidelity when:

- Students are actively engaged in using instructional resources that enhance student learning of mathematics

- Professional learning teams are investigating instructional resources that support curriculum and instruction

- The teacher is providing access to and using the appropriate resources

- Teachers clearly state the use of the instructional resources in lesson plans

- Teachers are using instructional resources to assess student learning

- Teachers are using the instructional resources appropriately

- Students use instructional resources to explore and deepen their understanding of concepts

Student Support Structures and Intensification Strategies

Raising achievement in mathematics for *every* student and effectively implementing the CCSSM in *every* classroom requires *a variety of intensification strategies be available to teachers to support the learning needs of struggling students.* We are using the term *intensification* instead of *intervention* to describe support for students outside the regular classroom. Rather than responding with an intervention strategy *after* students have failed, successful schools take a proactive stance by anticipating the learning needs of students that are not met within regular fifty- or sixty-minute class periods and by implementing strategies that *intensify* the learning experience. Using the term *intensification* also interrupts the mindset of pull-out programs as the only appropriate strategy for struggling students. Intensification strategies occur during the regular academic school year and

*Raising achievement in mathematics for **every** student and effectively implementing the CCSSM in **every** classroom requires **a variety of intensification strategies be available to teachers to support the learning needs of struggling students**.*

include additional learning time for targeted mathematics support before, during, or after school, with the intent of keeping students in the regular classroom.

To ensure that multiple intensification strategies are available to support the range of learning needs of struggling students, leaders and teams of leaders must:

- Consider and employ research-based support structures that will best fit the needs of the student population

- Identify students who need additional support, utilizing multiple data sources

- Ensure access to intensified learning opportunities for identified students

See the tool on page 77 in appendix C for a description of three intensification strategies that make a difference.

Consider and Employ Research-Based Support Structures

Two constructs should guide the implementation of any intensification strategy. First, successful strategies move students forward by expanding the learning experience. There is *no* evidence that content dilution strategies are effective. Content dilution strategies include courses such as those that progress students through the curriculum more slowly (such as taking algebra 1 over two years rather than one) or substituting courses with high-demand segments taken out (such as replacing the traditional geometry course with informal geometry that avoids asking students to construct their own mathematically rigorous arguments). The Stanford Research Institute project, *Principles for Improving Mathematics Learning in High-Poverty High Schools*, found no support for the effectiveness of dilution strategies either in their extensive review of the literature or in discussions with experts and practitioners. Therefore, strategies that dilute content for students are not included in *It's TIME*. The most successful strategies vary the time for learning, not the content expectations.

Second, no *single* intensification strategy is likely to be sufficient for a school to reach the goal of high achievement for all students in mathematics. Rather, this level of success requires schools to implement *multiple* intensification strategies that are comprehensive enough to address the diverse needs of learners. Plans to improve student achievement must recognize and respond to the fact that the reasons students struggle are diverse and therefore cannot all be remediated with a single solution. Furthermore, this constellation of support must sit inside a *system* that simultaneously works to maximize achievement growth through the variables of curriculum, pedagogy, climate, and teacher expectations in a knowledge-using and knowledge-building community. If we are to realize our goal of success for all students, a variety of intensification strategies *and* attention to each of these critical variables in our educational systems must be a priority. The bottom line is that while intensification strategies can be highly productive and are likely necessary, they are not sufficient.

Identify Students Who Need Additional Support

In most situations, identifying students who may benefit from an intensified learning experience does not require special tests or specially trained personnel. Schools can identify struggling students with data they already collect as part of their course placement procedures. Schools should use a variety of data sources with a team of educators including mathematics leaders, counselors, principals, and teachers. In particular, leaders and leadership teams should consider collecting input from teachers, parents, and students. Productive data sources include but are not limited to prior and current teachers, the student, parents, state assessment results, and benchmark or interim assessment results. Once potential candidates for these support strategies have been identified, teams can return to the data to determine what type and how much support will be needed to provide a successful learning experience for students.

Ensure Access to Intensified Learning Opportunities

More than a decade of research and experience suggests that leaders can increase achievement by ensuring that, in addition to high-quality classroom experiences, students also have access to intensified learning opportunities (Kilpatrick et al., 2001). Therefore, once mathematics leadership teams have looked and listened carefully to identify students who are not now succeeding in mathematics, the next step is to implement an effective support system that will *proactively* address the anticipated common learning needs of these students. The tool on page 77 in appendix C describes three intensification strategies with research-based evidence of effectiveness for improving student achievement. Each strategy is designed to meet a different learning need. Mathematics leadership teams should consider which might be most useful in their settings and work to adjust teaching schedules and courses to include these opportunities for additional learning time for students in need of support.

It will be evident that intensification strategies are being used effectively when:

- Schools and districts have a protocol for collecting and analyzing data to identify and assign students to appropriate support structures

- Schools have a comprehensive constellation of support structures based on the anticipated learning needs of struggling students

Summative Assessment Data

Raising achievement in mathematics for *every* student and effectively implementing the CCSSM in *every* classroom requires that schools *gather, collaboratively analyze, and effectively use a range of summative assessment data to plan and implement revisions at the student, lesson, unit, and program levels.* Using summative assessment data is the process of individually and collaboratively analyzing available data from tests, assessments, projects, surveys, and questionnaires and using these data to inform and implement

*Raising achievement in mathematics for **every** student and effectively implementing the CCSSM in **every** classroom requires that schools **gather, collaboratively analyze, and effectively use a range of summative assessment data to plan and implement revisions at the student, lesson, unit, and program levels.***

To ensure an effective use of summative assessment data:

- *Analyze the structure and context of summative assessments, and disaggregate the data*

- *Ensure that teachers understand summative assessments and can interpret the data*

- *Create opportunities for professional development based on learning gaps*

revisions and improvements to curriculum, instruction, professional development, and assessments.

To ensure an effective use of summative assessment data, leaders and teams of leaders must:

- Analyze the structure and context of summative assessments, and disaggregate the data reflecting performance of subpopulations and content topics as input for instructional planning and improved student learning

- Ensure that teachers understand summative assessments and can interpret the data

- Create opportunities for professional development based on learning gaps the disaggregation of summative assessment data identify

Analyze the Structure and Context of Summative Assessments, and Disaggregate the Data

Summative assessment is the process for determining what and how much students have learned over a specified time. The enactment of No Child Left Behind legislation in 2001 led to an increased focus on summative assessment. Research studies supported by the U.S. Department of Education and private entities helped document the development of summative assessment tools and tests such as state-level minimum-performance tests and nationally-normed assessments as measures of school performance. The state and national instruments teachers use to collect such data and how the data are used have been the focus of many research studies, state and federal government mandates, professional development sessions, and educational "how to" publications from 2003 to 2014. NCSM's 2008 *The PRIME Leadership Framework* provides a rubric (see page 80 in appendix C) that establishes outcomes for assessment leadership and describes expectations for both summative and formative classroom assessments.

Academic leaders are responsible for understanding the process of assessment and assisting and guiding classroom teachers through the various assessment strategies, which include using assessment data to report student progress and, more importantly, to inform instruction. While many educators as well as the general public are focused on high-stakes tests, it is important for administrators and teachers to understand the utility of such assessments but also understand that the teacher's informal assessment of student understanding and day-to-day performance frames instruction and guides learning trajectories throughout the school year.

Teachers should design and implement student assessments around the content they expect students to know and be able to do. As states continue to adopt the CCSSM, the mathematics content students are expected to know has taken a dramatic shift. The extent to which the CCSSM is adopted and implemented at the classroom level determines students' potential for success on aligned assessments regardless of the source of assessment—PARCC or SBAC.

Instructional leaders should be able to help classroom teachers understand and align the content of the CCSSM and classroom practice with assessment practices. The National Council on Teacher Quality identifies three essential domains teachers should take into account for effective assessment and assessment preparation (Greenberg & Walsh, 2012).

1. Assessment literacy: How to measure student performance using assessments

2. Analytical skills: How to analyze student performance data from such assessments

3. Instructional decision making: How to use student performance data from assessments to plan instruction

The report summarizes curricula collected from teacher preparation programs across the United States. The findings suggest that fewer than 3 percent of the identified teacher education programs provide an adequate program whereby teacher education candidates can experience work in the area of student assessment. Such findings clearly point out that most teachers and teacher education candidates are woefully underprepared in the area of assessing and using assessment data.

Ensure That Teachers Understand Summative Assessments and Can Interpret the Data

Instructional leaders in schools must ensure that every classroom teacher understands the purposes of summative assessments and is able to interpret data the assessment provides. As defined in *The PRIME Leadership Framework* (NCSM, 2008) and further supported by Tim Kanold (2012b) and colleagues, effective classroom leaders use summative data to evaluate mathematics grade-level, course, and program effectiveness. In its simplest form, summative assessments inform the teacher about student learning and understanding and provide an objective process for evaluating individual student performance. Beyond the individual classroom, summative assessments have been a common U.S. practice for many years. Such assessments may include, but are not limited to, large-scale assessments with data most often being norm referenced from tests that are designed around student objectives common to a region or across many states. Educators and educational researchers who use and interpret summative assessment data must also consider the construct of the test, the alignment of the assessment with the core curriculum, and external factors such as reliability and validity of the instrument.

Norm-referenced assessments are more global in scope, cover a wider range of content, and provide data that allow comparison with similar demographic and state or regional groups. Schools normally administer such standardized (norm-referenced) assessments near the end of a school year, which provide a wealth of data for school use as well as for reporting to the public.

Research from Brian Stecher et al. (2008) describes practices of classrooms and schools using summative data. The findings in this research indicate that state assessments and data requirements from the No Child Left Behind Act (NCLB) of 2001 have led to an increased use of the assessment results in many classrooms. When those data were disaggregated at the classroom level, and teachers used the data to identify areas in which students failed to perform at proficient standards and then used that information to inform instruction, student performance improved. Additionally, teachers stated that data from the state assessments were used to improve curriculum, individualize instruction, and identify the need to enhance their own subject matter knowledge and teaching skills. Teachers must understand the different information that norm-referenced and criterion-referenced assessments provide and the format for reporting both.

Create Opportunities for Professional Development Based on Learning Gaps

Professional development aimed at ensuring teachers are able to read and interpret summative assessments is a common need across the United States. A school or district must provide training for data usage to ensure teachers use it effectively, as Stecher et al. (2008) note.

In addition to the curriculum changes taking place in schools adopting the CCSSM, schools also face changes to assessments. As noted previously, two large-scale assessment projects, PARCC and SBAC, are designing the first multistate high-stakes common assessments to report on U.S. student performance. Both consortia plan to measure student performance and provide summative data that can inform instruction based on the CCSSM. As explained on the PARCC website,

> In spring 2014, the PARCC Field Test will be administered to over one million students across PARCC states. The PARCC Field Test represents a critical milestone in PARCC's work toward building assessments for the 2014–15 school year, and will give students and local educators the opportunity to experience the administration of PARCC assessments. (Partnership for Assessment of Readiness for College and Careers, 2013)

For Smarter Balanced states,

> Students in grades 3–8 and 11—along with a small sample of students in grades 9 and 10—will participate in the Field Test. Administered online, the Field Test will closely resemble the summative assessment that students will participate in during the spring of 2015. (Smarter Balanced Assessment Consortium, 2012)

Instructional leaders must keep teachers informed as to the development of these large-scale assessments and be mindful of the trends that seem to be emerging. Resources are available from both PARCC and SBAC that will help ease the transition into the assessment format and the rigor of the assessments. Visit www.parcconline.org or www.smarterbalanced.org for more information and sample assessment items. Both of these websites provide sample assessment items and a context for developing additional items consistent with the CCSSM. As the date approaches for pilot testing, and then full implementation, educational leaders should keep abreast of the progress of item development and proposed assessment and reporting strategies.

The use of summative assessment data from PARCC and SBAC at the classroom level is key to improved student performance. Thus, it remains a function of instructional leaders to provide those skills through professional development and continued teacher education. Changes in curriculum, which lead to changes in the nature and structure of assessments, demand that teacher leaders become proactive in developing and maintaining the competence of teachers in the administration and interpretation of summative assessments.

It will be evident that summative assessments are shaping student performance when:

- Teams of teachers collaboratively review summative assessment data and use the data to plan curricular and instructional adjustments

- All summative assessments used to monitor student performance and program effectiveness are tightly aligned with the mathematics content being taught

Visit **go.solution-tree.com/mathematics** for links to relevant online resources related to the topics discussed in this chapter.

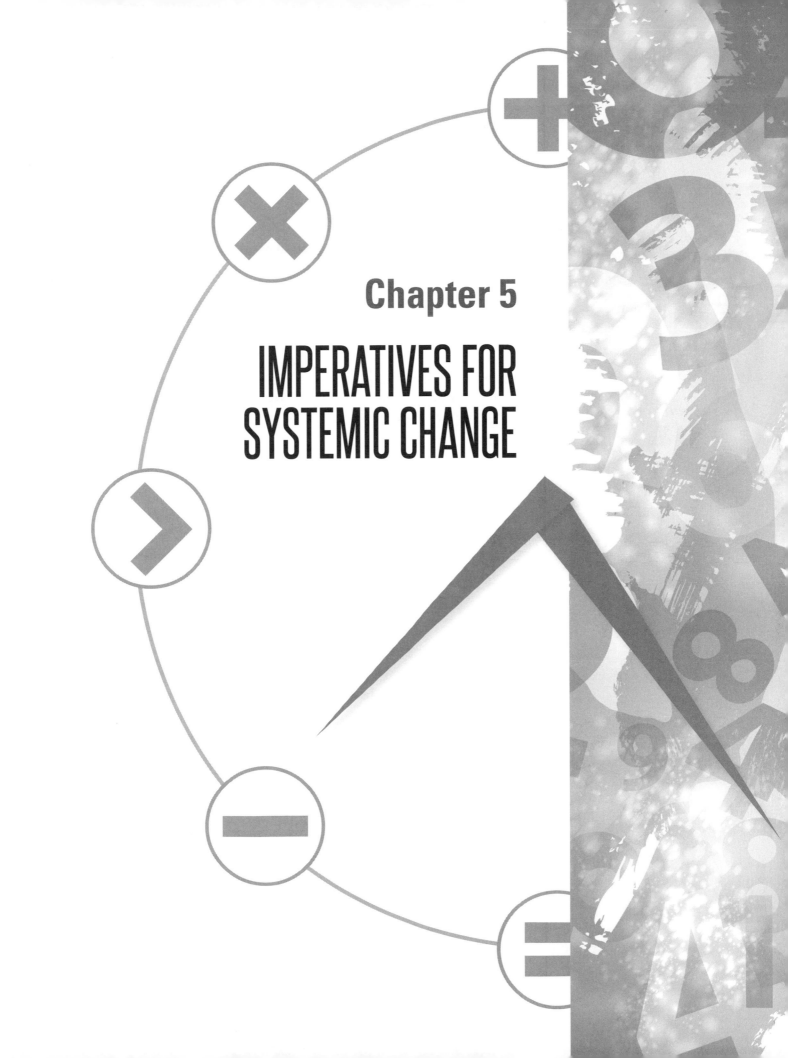

Chapter 5

IMPERATIVES FOR SYSTEMIC CHANGE

In this chapter, we turn to three final, and too often missing, imperatives for reaching our goals: (1) ongoing job-embedded opportunities for professional learning, (2) diverse structures and adequate time for professional collaboration, and (3) opportunities for coaching.

Professional Learning

Raising achievement in mathematics for *every* student and effectively implementing the CCSSM in *every* classroom requires *extensive and ongoing opportunities for teachers to enhance their own professional learning and to build their capacity to reach all students*. Professional learning refers to both the individual and the collective experiences that contribute to the growth of knowledge and skill throughout one's career.

To ensure that there are extensive and ongoing opportunities for teachers to enhance their own professional learning and to build their capacity to reach all students, leaders and teams of leaders must:

- Recognize the diversity of skills

- Provide differentiated learning experiences while maintaining an identified focus

- Capture and monitor teacher learning outcomes

- Introduce and reinforce purposefully selected new learning

- Reflect on failures and successes

- Disseminate new learning

Recognize the Diversity of Skills

Teachers bring varied levels of experience, knowledge, skills, and beliefs to their professional learning experiences. These variations impact how teachers plan and present mathematics lessons. For example, a novice teacher may possess technology skills; however, he or she may lack actual classroom management experience. Meanwhile, a veteran teacher with many years of experience may not have technology-based expertise yet might have skill in lesson design. With this understanding of varied expertise, the need for collaboration becomes obvious and vital. Leaders and leadership teams must understand and utilize the strengths of their teacher colleagues and specifically address individual professional learning needs.

Provide Differentiated Learning Experiences While Maintaining an Identified Focus

Leaders who recognize that teachers have different levels of experience, knowledge, skills, and beliefs must provide professional learning in a variety of instructional formats appropriate to the teachers' needs, including lesson study, book studies, video analysis, gallery walks, task analyses, learning communities, and instructional rounds. Professional development occurs best when adult learning is differentiated for varied purposes, interests, and career

*Raising achievement in mathematics for **every** student and effectively implementing the CCSSM in **every** classroom requires **extensive and ongoing opportunities for teachers to enhance their own professional learning and to build their capacity to reach all students**.*

stages (Hull, Miles, & Balka, 2012). Leaders and teachers collaboratively determine a professional learning focus based on current research, needs assessments, classroom observations, and teacher input. For example, focus areas might include student discourse, challenging and engaging problems, or data analyses.

Capture and Monitor Teacher Learning Outcomes

Successful professional development requires evaluation and feedback from skilled practitioners with expertise in teaching methods (Elmore & Burney, 1997). The evaluation process determines if and in what ways the professional learning was successful. Reflection on the evaluation results is an important contributor to continuous improvement. This process requires thoughtful and careful design based on sound principles and strategies. During the evaluation process, teams should ask the following questions (Loucks-Horsley et al., 2003, p. 27):

- What are the goals or desired outcomes of professional learning?

- How is the accomplishment of the outcomes assessed?

- In what ways are a professional development initiative and its participants' change over time acknowledged and evaluated?

- How might evaluation be recognized as a learning experience in and of itself?

Introduce and Reinforce Purposefully Selected New Learning

As Susan Loucks-Horsley and her colleagues (2003) explain, "Professional developers can foster collaboration through structuring experiences of shared learning and special skill development" (p. 94). In order to be successful, professional development has to be linked closely to the learning of the students in the classroom with considerations to the content, context, and process. As Linda Darling-Hammond and her colleagues explain:

> As in any professional development enterprise, it is also critically important that the instructional practices promoted through coaching are themselves more effective for the goals and circumstances in which they are being used than the practices teachers are otherwise using. The content of professional learning matters as much as the process by which it is transmitted. (Darling-Hammond, Wei, Andree, Richardson, & Orphanos, 2009, p. 12)

In other words, what Darling-Hammond and her colleagues are describing is a culture of professional learning that embraces risk taking.

Effective professional development for teachers of mathematics (Darling-Hammond et al., 2009; Smith, 2011):

- Is intensive, continuing, connected, and supportive to the ongoing work of teaching

To ensure that there are extensive and ongoing opportunities for teachers to enhance their professional learning:

- *Recognize the diversity of skills*

- *Provide differentiated learning experiences*

- *Capture and monitor teacher learning outcomes*

- *Introduce and reinforce purposefully selected new learning*

- *Reflect on failures and successes*

- *Disseminate new learning*

- Focuses on student learning as the ultimate goal

- Is grounded in mathematics content

- Models and reflects the pedagogy of research-affirmed best practice

- Has shared beliefs, values, and visions, specifically aligned with school improvement objectives

- Develops robust working connections and collaborations among teachers

- Considers teachers' contexts

- Uses teachers' knowledge and expertise

- Offers supportive conditions and environment

- Includes shared and supportive leadership

Shifting professional development structures from large group presentations to job-embedded and job-related professional learning is essential for raising professionalism and reducing isolation.

Reflect on Failures and Successes

Levels of success will vary as teachers engage in learning opportunities. Some teaching methods will undoubtedly be more effective than others. Through the process of reflection, continued professional learning occurs. Lessons learned are shared through a process that invites a critical review to determine effective strategies for teaching and learning mathematics. In the process, all involved increase their own knowledge of content and effective pedagogy. When teachers collaboratively share their experiences with a group of colleagues as part of professional learning, they receive important feedback and support that helps inform their actions. As stated in *The PRIME Leadership Framework* (NCSM, 2008), "Communities of adult learning are the building blocks that will establish a new foundation in America's schools" (p. 3).

Disseminate New Learning

As James Hiebert (1999) explains:

> Fruitful opportunities to learn new instructional strategies share several core features: (a) ongoing collaboration of teachers for purposes of planning with (b) the explicit goal of improving students' achievement of clear learning goals, (c) anchored by attention to students' thinking, the curriculum, and pedagogy, with (d) access to alternative ideas and methods and opportunities to observe these in action and to reflect on the reasons for their effectiveness. (p. 15)

Characteristics of professional development that relate to positive outcomes for teachers and students include the following: a focus on content knowledge, active learning, collective participation, contact hours, coherence, and enhanced knowledge and skills (Desimone,

Porter, Garet, Yoon, & Birman, 2001). Improving students' learning outcomes requires that professional development experiences be grounded in the belief that "excellence in mathematics education requires equity—high expectations and strong support for all students" (NCTM, 2000, p. 12). Professional development must provide opportunities for teachers to consider the impact of their teaching practices on what students learn, how students learn it, and the ways in which they can support *all* students—regardless of success or previous lack of success—in learning rigorous and significant mathematics.

It will be evident that professional learning is effective when:

- Outcomes for professional learning are related to mathematical content knowledge, pedagogical knowledge, and specialized content knowledge

- Peer dialogue and feedback support classroom endeavors

- Collegial sharing of learning experiences occurs inside and outside the school

- All teachers participate in professional learning opportunities

- Teachers develop a coherent plan to document professional goals and progress toward them

- Teams predicate learning opportunities on what they know from research-affirmed best practices for professional development in mathematical content knowledge, pedagogical knowledge, and specialized content knowledge

- Teachers have data-informed conversations with colleagues about what is working and what is not working in order to ensure that all students are achieving

- Educators celebrate and share individual and collective successes

Collaborative Structures

Raising achievement in mathematics for *every* student and effectively implementing the CCSSM in *every* classroom requires *robust, well-functioning collaborative structures, including administrative teams, academic leader teams, and grade-level or course-specific teams.* Collaborative structures refer to teams of educators ultimately focused on student achievement. Each team functions for a unique purpose and at different levels within a district. In each case, the purpose is to focus on the critical aspects of teaching and learning mathematics. Administrative teams focus on those priorities that implement the vision of the organization. Academic team leaders support the implementation of instructional practices while working with grade-level or course-specific collaborative teams. These teams collaboratively identify learning targets, plan meaningful lessons that promote student learning, create common assessments, analyze student work, and support each other

*Raising achievement in mathematics for **every** student and effectively implementing the CCSSM in **every** classroom requires **robust, well-functioning collaborative structures, including administrative teams, academic leader teams, and grade-level or course-specific teams.***

in making improvements that raise student achievement. Collaborative structures are necessary to create and support changes in schools and districts.

To ensure that there are robust, well-functioning collaborative structures, leaders and teams of leaders must:

- Cultivate a professional culture of transparency, collaboration, and mutual respect within every school and mathematics department

- Ensure that districts or schools establish administrative teams that lead the development, implementation, and monitoring of a vision of teaching and learning throughout the system

- Establish academic leader teams that develop, implement, and monitor the effective teaching practices and district policies that deliver the vision throughout the system

- Establish grade-level or course-specific teacher teams that function as the engines for change in schools and districts

Cultivate a Professional Culture

Teacher collaboration is a professional obligation. It is an obligation that uses the power of the exchange of ideas to enhance teaching practices and thus provide opportunities for professional learning and growth. Collaborative teams harness their energy to focus on student learning; this focus removes the spotlight from the teacher as the center of learning and places that light on students' understandings. Collaborative teacher teams develop an interdependence that enables their work to be efficient and effective. These team members feel responsible for all the students who the team's efforts impact—not just those students who are in their individual classes.

Teachers collaborate on planning effective lessons and observe and monitor students' progress toward specific learning targets through common assessments and formative assessment strategies. Teacher teams adjust lessons based on information collected from these assessment strategies. Teams intentionally identify learning needs of students who have demonstrated mastery as well as those who need re-engagement with a particular concept. To function effectively and efficiently takes considerable effort and time. Collaborative teams tend to progress through stages of development, from social chatter to reflecting on effective teaching strategies and identifying action steps for improvement. See figure 5.1 for information on the cyclical work of collaborative teams, and see page 81 in appendix C for a description of the stages of team development.

Teacher teams plan meaningful tasks and opportunities for students to collaborate. Meaningful tasks require that students work to make sense of the context, apply what they know, and have opportunities to engage in the Standards for Mathematical Practice. According to Tim Kanold (2013) and his colleagues, "A growing body of research links students' engagement in higher-level cognitive demand tasks to overall increases in mathematics learning, not just in the ability to solve problems (Resnick, 2006)" (p. 64).

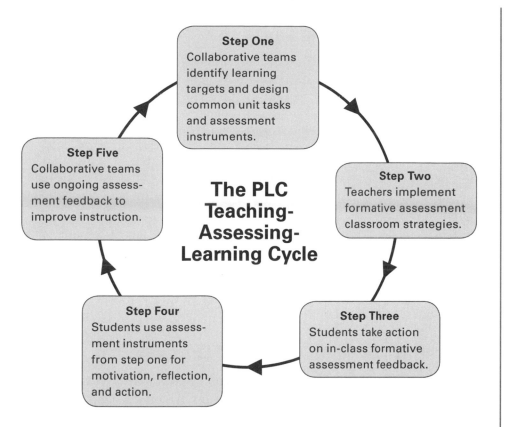

Figure 5.1: The PLC teaching-assessing-learning cycle.
Visit **go.solution-tree.com/mathematics** *for a reproducible version of this figure.*
Source: Kanold, 2012a. Used with permission.

The work of collaborative teacher teams takes time, planning, and effort. As a group, teachers raise their standards and improve their practice for the benefit of improved student understanding. As Kanold (2013) and colleagues explain:

> A shared understanding and agreement of what student learning looks like and sounds like leads to greater coherence in the instruction and expectations of mathematical learning by all students of the course as well as by every teacher for the course. (p. 63)

Ensure Districts or Schools Establish Administrative Teams

Administrative teams consist of administrators who collaborate with stakeholders to develop and support the implementation of a common vision for the school or district. Administrative teams should be expected to:

- Identify and establish priorities for the implementation of the vision

- Articulate and support the identified action steps leading to the vision for the district

- Establish priorities and direct resources, including time, expertise, funds, and materials, toward the implementation of the vision

- Ensure that the professional learning opportunities provided align with action steps supporting the vision

- Participate in professional conversations alongside teachers in monitoring the focus and planned actions toward improving student learning

- Meet with families and the community at large to describe the curricular and assessment goals

- Look for local, state, and nationwide partners and models

Administrative teams focus on removing the barriers that inhibit the work of academic team leaders and teacher teams. The foundation that enables administrators to effectively support teacher teams includes *reciprocal accountability*. Reciprocal accountability means that as administrators clarify expectations and establish goals, they also hold themselves accountable for creating an environment and building the capacity to successfully meet those challenges (DuFour, DuFour, Eaker, & Many, 2010).

Establish Academic Leader Teams

Academic leader teams develop, implement, and monitor the effective teaching practices and district policies that deliver vision throughout the system. These teams should:

- Articulate and communicate the meaning of effective instruction

- Support teacher teams as they expand their repertoire of skills to improve student engagement

- Guarantee that there is dedicated meeting time within the school workday

- Ensure alignment of the implemented content at each grade level with the CCSSM

- Provide structure and guidance to ensure that teams are focused on the correct work

- Monitor the work of the collaborative teams by analyzing data from common assessments and conducting periodic reviews of the team's goals and action steps

- Offer professional learning opportunities for teachers that target the specific needs of the team as well as of the individual teacher

- Identify the appropriate professional learning model (lesson study, collegial classroom visits, or analysis of student work) for the teacher teams to use

Academic team leaders must "act to remove the barriers of teacher isolation, create the conditions and structures for teacher grade or course level collaboration during the *normal work* day, and establish training for the development of crucial conversation skills among all adults" (NCSM, 2007, p. 2). Academic team leaders work to build consensus with teachers

As administrators clarify expectations and establish goals, they also hold themselves accountable for creating an environment and building the capacity to successfully meet those challenges.

on the definition of effective instruction. Additionally, they offer resources and videos and model lessons that enable teachers to study the components of effective instruction. Academic team leaders also monitor the work of collaborative course- or grade-level teams by conducting meetings to focus on assessment data and then support teachers as they plan next steps to deepen students' learning.

Establish Grade-Level or Course-Specific Teacher Teams

Another critical collaborative structure focuses on grade-level or course-specific teacher teams. Teams of leaders launch, nurture, and support these teacher teams as they:

- Identify and define the learning targets for every unit

- Establish common assessments

- Work collaboratively to incorporate mathematical tasks that enable students to develop the habits of mind described in the Standards for Mathematical Practice

- Provide ample opportunities for students to discuss, collaborate, and collectively build their understanding

- Identify the formative assessments for teachers to use during the lessons

- Plan how to respond when students have not been successful and anticipate providing opportunities for students who have demonstrated mastery early

- Target lesson plans based on students' individual understanding

- Reflect on the unit, based on assessment results, and take appropriate action

A growing body of evidence exists supporting the idea that teacher collaboration improves student achievement (Borko, 2004; Gearhart & Omundson, 2008; Goddard, Goddard, & Tschannen-Moran, 2007). Schmoker (2005) notes that "the right kind of continuous, structured teacher collaboration improves the quality of teaching and pays big, often immediate, dividends in student learning and professional morale in virtually any setting" (p. 177).

It will be evident that implementation of collaborative structures is happening when:

- All stakeholders know the vision and can articulate it

- Teams discuss assessment results and create action steps to improve student learning

- Student achievement goals are met and re-established for continued improvement

- Teachers broaden, deepen, and enhance their instructional practices

- Students' level of engagement increases throughout the class period

- Teachers request professional learning opportunities

Coaching

Raising achievement in mathematics for *every* student and effectively implementing the CCSSM in *every* classroom requires that *knowledgeable and trained coaches support instruction improvement and professional collaboration in every school*. Mathematics coaches are individuals who are well-versed in mathematics content and pedagogy and who work directly with classroom teachers to improve student learning of mathematics (Hull, Balka, & Miles, 2009).

To ensure that knowledgeable and trained coaches support instructional improvement and professional collaboration in every school, leaders and teams of leaders must:

- Advocate for the critical role of mathematics coaches

- Define the responsibilities of coaches and protect their opportunities to carry out these responsibilities

- Provide coaches with professional learning opportunities that strengthen mathematical content and pedagogical knowledge while providing appropriate information on gathering, analyzing, and interpreting data

- Deploy coaches strategically in schools, ensuring that the number of schools receiving support is realistic and based on the number of coaches

- Provide opportunities for mathematics coaches to collaborate regularly and share their expertise, experiences, and best practices

Advocate for Mathematics Coaches

Coaching has been shown to be an effective method of changing teacher practices and improving student achievement. There are several coaching models that leaders can use, including: (1) cognitive coaching (Costa & Garmston, 2002), (2) content-focused coaching (West & Staub, 2003), (3) instructional coaching (Knight, 2007), and (4) pedagogical content coaching (Foster, 2007). In all models, coaches work directly with teachers to change instructional practices, which in turn improves student achievement. The role of coaches is vital in creating opportunities to implement new curricular innovations that impact student learning. By building trust through coach-teacher relationships, coaches encourage teachers to be risk takers in moving toward effective instructional practices.

Research findings (Campbell, 2012) on mathematics coaching are positive. In studies of the *Silicon Valley Mathematics Initiative* (Pack, 2008a) mathematics coaching improved the pedagogy of teachers and the mathematics learning of students.

Traditionally, mathematics coaches have worked in schools and school districts in which their responsibilities were unclear or nonexistent to them and to their teachers. Administrators provided a universal charge: improve student learning of mathematics, and close the achievement gap.

Define the Responsibilities of Coaches

As their roles have evolved, many coaches have become involved in teacher evaluation. This particular responsibility has created serious issues of trust between coaches and teachers—issues that thwart the overall goal of improved student achievement in mathematics. Consequently, administrators must establish an acceptable set of responsibilities for coaches—one that does not include teacher evaluation. District and school administrators must support coaches in their efforts to improve student achievement in mathematics.

Coaches should:

- Work with teachers in and out of the classroom to co-plan and co-teach lessons, and then reflect on the lessons afterward

- Share best practice research through professional learning opportunities

- Monitor mathematics program implementation

- Oversee curriculum and instructional resources

- Inform mathematics instruction using student work, assessment data, and benchmark tests

Provide Coaches With Professional Learning Opportunities

To help teachers understand that the CCSSM or state mathematics content improves instructional strategies and increases student achievement, mathematics coaches must have a deep understanding of the content and the connections between content areas. For example, consider these questions: What are the big ideas of algebra and geometry? How do the big ideas in elementary school translate into the big ideas in middle school and high school? What is the mathematics needed to be mathematically literate in 21st century society? Coaches must also understand the relationship between the local mathematics standards and the state-adopted standards or the CCSSM.

Deploy Coaches Strategically

Coaches are placed in schools to provide on-site professional learning that addresses mathematical content and pedagogy in order to enhance instruction and to improve student achievement. A critical component for this to occur is the positioning of specialists who have strong mathematical content and pedagogical knowledge, who understand their responsibilities, and who can apply the tenets of skilled coaching. However, to maximize impact, these knowledgeable specialists need to work collaboratively with supportive principals as instructional leaders in their schools. They must have

To ensure that knowledgeable and trained coaches support instructional improvement and professional collaboration in every school:

- *Advocate for the critical role of mathematics coaches*

- *Define the responsibilities of coaches and protect their opportunities to carry out these responsibilities*

- *Provide coaches with professional learning opportunities*

- *Deploy coaches strategically in schools*

- *Provide opportunities for mathematics coaches to collaborate regularly*

direct contact with classroom teachers, establishing a professional rapport and sense of trust with those teachers.

The ultimate goal of coaching is to improve students' mathematics learning. To implement the CCSSM, a mathematics coach available for every classroom will not only make a teacher's job easier but also provide an invaluable support for teachers. Teams of leaders must interpret data to drive change initiatives and then strategically place coaches in classrooms to co-plan and co-teach with teachers to improve student achievement.

Provide Opportunities for Coaches to Collaborate

Finally, successful mathematics coaches establish strong professional relationships among their leadership team members. Their everyday actions in the pursuit of achieving student learning of mathematics provide a sense of confidence and trust among colleagues.

It will be evident that mathematics coaches are making a difference when they:

- Work with teachers in and out of the classroom to improve mathematics achievement

- Manage and regulate professional development related to mathematics content and pedagogy

- Manage curriculum and instructional resources

- Monitor implementation of an aligned mathematics curriculum

- Work to develop and improve a coherent school or district mathematics program by focusing on its strengths and reducing its weaknesses

- Maintain and provide best instructional practice research for teachers

- Build collaborative teams and networks involving teachers, administrators, curriculum coordinators, mathematics specialists, and mathematics coaches

- Inform mathematics instruction by gathering, analyzing, and interpreting data from student work, local benchmark tests and assessments, end-of-course tests, and state assessments

Raising achievement in mathematics for every student is the ultimate goal for teachers. In order to help students learn efficiently and effectively, teachers must continue their own learning throughout their teaching careers. Professional learning, whether it takes place individually or collectively, contributes to the growth of knowledge and skill that a teacher needs to be successful. Job-embedded opportunities, diverse professional learning structures, adequate time for building content and pedagogical knowledge, and meaningful opportunities for coaching all contribute to the knowledge that teachers need. Visit **go.solution-tree.com/mathematics** for links to relevant online resources related to the topics discussed in this chapter.

Chapter 6

SHARED PRODUCTIVE CULTURE

F inally, we must acknowledge one critical precursor at the heart of raising achievement in mathematics for *every* student and effectively implementing the CCSSM in *every* classroom: the development of a productive, inclusive, cohesive, and positive school culture. A shared productive culture is necessary to successfully carry out the overarching themes, supportive conditions, and imperatives to effectively implement the CCSSM and raise student achievement.

The shared beliefs, purpose, core values, and priorities that drive the thinking and actions of people within a school community comprise the school culture. Culture is an ongoing, shifting, dynamic process. It is the responsibility of leaders and teams of leaders to nurture and intentionally shape the culture in every school setting.

According to Kent Peterson and Terrence Deal (1998), leaders and teams of leaders must attend to the following elements of a school's culture.

- Communicating agreed-on core values, priorities, and purpose in what is said and done

- Respecting diversity, different viewpoints, and traditions among staff, parents, and students

- Developing actions, timelines, and strategies for monitoring progress toward the agreed-on priorities and core values

A productive school culture depends on strong leadership and purpose and must align with the school vision. You know you are in a school with a productive culture when there is trust, transparency, collaboration, and a focus on quality and accountability. In fact, until all members of a school community are treated with dignity and respect, there will not be enough trust for transparency. Until the school environment has greater transparency and openness, educators will have few incentives to collaborate. Until educators effectively collaborate and fully understand that learning (our students' as well as our own) is a socially mediated process, the overall quality of our work is unlikely to significantly improve. Finally, until educators build the foundation for a productive culture, their school communities will lack sufficient support and meaningful accountability that ensure every student has the opportunity to learn.

Leaders influence school culture by establishing norms and providing a clear, common direction for what is important and needs to be accomplished. In a dynamic, productive culture, people are treated with respect and dignity. The environment is one of transparency and risk taking in which the norm is collaboration and finding solutions rather than isolation and making excuses. In a dynamic, productive culture, leaders hold each other and teachers accountable for team decisions. Additionally, leaders pay close attention to all aspects of the mathematics program and develop protocols to address conflict.

A strong shared productive culture exists when there is:

- Commitment to academic success for all students and to social justice—Leaders must design, implement, and evaluate all components of the K–12 mathematics program to ensure teacher effectiveness and success for all students. In a culture of success with

Culture is an ongoing, shifting, dynamic process. It is the responsibility of leaders and teams of leaders to nurture and intentionally shape the culture in every school setting.

a commitment to social justice, every student will graduate from high school with the procedural and conceptual mathematics knowledge necessary for future workforce training and college academic coursework. Additionally, they will have expertise and confidence to understand and address pressing issues in their community and in the larger world.

- Accountability—Leaders must hold teachers and other stakeholders accountable to make decisions that support the shared vision of teaching and learning mathematics. Teachers must feel valued and comfortable with peer observations and inquiries into personal practice. In a shared culture of accountability, leaders and teachers recognize personal strengths and weaknesses and embrace the need for continuous improvement and professional learning.

- Celebration of accomplishments—Leaders must help teachers recognize students for their perseverance and academic success, no matter how small, in learning mathematics. A strong, productive culture celebrates staff innovation and student accomplishment while setting new goals. The school community recognizes and celebrates parents for supporting their children and the school in the pursuit of excellence in mathematics for all students.

Throughout this book we have made a case for leaders with a vision of teaching and learning of mathematics. To support the vision, non-negotiable imperatives were introduced to maximize instructional effectiveness, opportunities to learn for *every* student, and effective implementation of the CCSSM in *every* classroom. Realizing these imperatives will help ensure that:

- Teachers understand the mathematics content that they expect students to learn

- Teachers understand what teaching approaches best fit the content and how to best organize the content's elements for effective teaching

- Teachers understand the content they are expected to teach to best sequence, connect, and situate it within learning progressions

- Teachers consistently implement effective, research-affirmed instructional practices and formative assessment practices in every classroom

- Instructional resources support the planning, implementation, and assessment of high-quality lessons; are aligned with the content and practices of the CCSSM; create excitement and motivation; and are developmentally appropriate

- A wide variety of intensification strategies is available to support the learning needs of struggling students

- Educators gather, collaboratively analyze, and effectively use a range of summative assessment data to plan and implement revisions at the student, lesson, unit, and program levels

- Leaders provide extensive and ongoing opportunities for teachers to enhance their own professional learning and to build their capacity to reach all students

- Educators create and support robust, well-functioning collaborative structures—including administrative teams, academic team leaders, and grade-level or course-specific teams

- Knowledgeable and trained coaches support professional collaboration and improvement of instruction in every school

These are the essential elements of the leader's agenda and are the non-negotiable program components that need to be in place if we are to meet our goals of far higher and broader levels of mathematics achievement.

Every leader and policymaker responsible for mathematics education must:

- Initially conduct an honest self-appraisal of the degree to which the preceding list of elements are or are not in place and the degree to which they are implemented effectively

- Collaboratively build and prioritize a detailed action plan that ensures each element is in place at a high level in every department, school, and district

- Designate responsibility for implementing the plan and identify specific actions and timelines for this implementation

- Establish a process of monitoring, reviewing, and revising the plan

From planning to implementation to revision, the leadership framework for the CCSSM provides a foundation for the shared productive culture of accountability, success and commitment to social justice, and celebration of accomplishment that are the essential prerequisites to effective, consistent, and impactful implementation of the letter and spirit of the CCSSM and significantly higher levels of student achievement we have promised our students, their parents, and society at large.

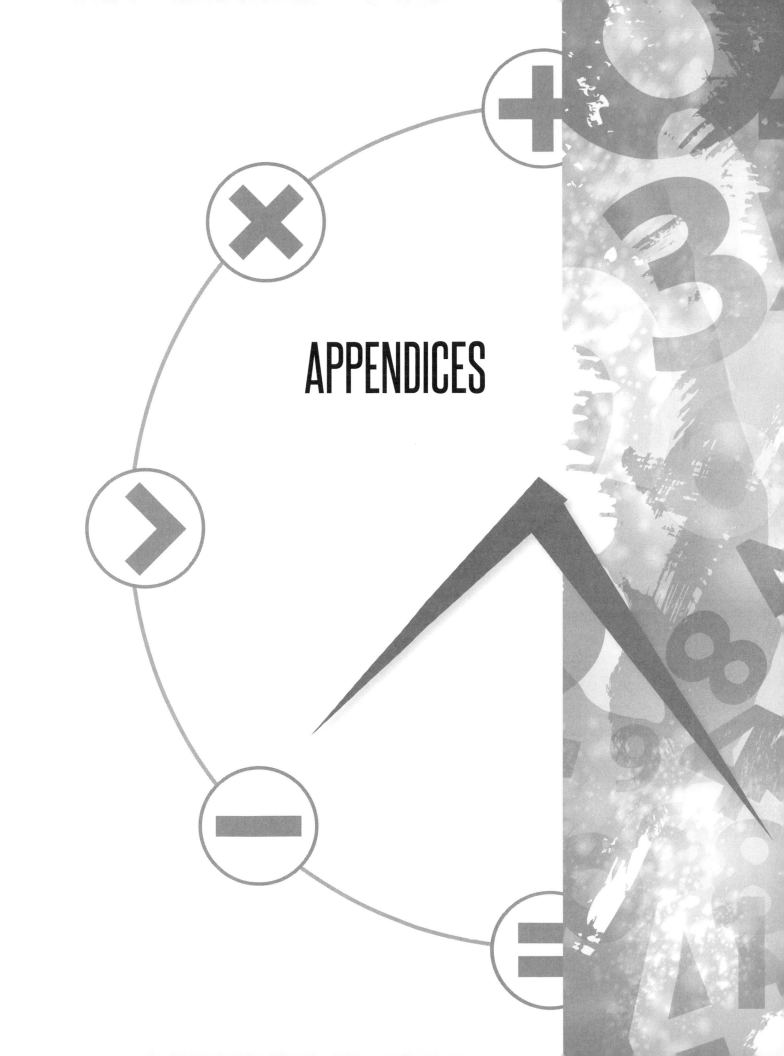

APPENDICES

Appendix A
Characteristics of a Standards-Based Mathematics Classroom

Source: Massachusetts Department of Elementary and Secondary Education, 2009. The Characteristics of a Standards-Based Mathematics Classroom document is included by permission of the Massachusetts Department of Elementary and Secondary Education. Inclusion does not constitute endorsement of this book or any other publication. The Characteristics of a Standards-Based Mathematics Classroom document is posted at: http://www.doe.mass.edu/omste/news07/mathclass_char.pdf#search=%22Mathematics%22 .

To support efforts to improve the teaching and learning of mathematics across the state, in the summer of 2005 the Massachusetts Department of Elementary and Secondary Education (ESE) launched the Comprehensive School Reform Math Initiative. Each district participating in this initiative received grant funding to support a full-time staff position dedicated to leadership of the district's math initiative. These leaders, in cooperation with ESE, come together regularly as the Math Support Specialist (MSS) Network to share ideas, resources, and strategies related to K-8 mathematics education reform.

ESE's Mathematics Targeted Assistance team and the MSS Network participants have developed a shared vision of standards-based mathematics teaching and learning to guide this new collaboration. Based on this vision, we have articulated the characteristics of an effective standards-based mathematics classroom and their corresponding indicators to serve as a reference for instructional planning and observation. This document represents the present state of this work. It is intended to support activities that advance standards-based educational practice, including formal study, dialogue and discussion, classroom observations, and other professional development activities.

A Shared Vision of Standards-Based Mathematics Teaching and Learning

Standards-based mathematics teaching and learning is a cooperative effort by teachers and students to actively engage in purposeful learning experiences that stimulate curiosity, enjoyment, and deep understanding of the mathematical concepts outlined in the Massachusetts Mathematics Curriculum Framework. Teachers and students are knowledgeable about learning objectives, and have ownership of and are accountable for learning outcomes.

Characteristics of a Standards-Based Mathematics Classroom

The original 2006 document developed in collaboration with ESE and the Math Support Specialists network has been modified to increase its sensitivity for use in classrooms providing math instruction to English Language Learners. In this draft version, additions to the document are in a bold italic font. While most of the original (and many additional) indicators represent good practice for all students, many are imperative for effective teaching and learning for ELL students. The indicators are intended to be suggestive, not exhaustive, identifying what effective implementation of the associated characteristic might look like in classroom practice. It is expected that this document will provide helpful, practical guidance for those who teach and those who support instruction for English Language Learners.

I. Student Learning Standards

Characteristic 1.1: Learning Standards Are Evident

Characteristic:

The mathematics learning standards being addressed in the lesson are evident and clear to the students.

Indicators:

- ***Teacher introduces standards using language and/or representations appropriate to the age and/or English language proficiency of students.***

- Standards are clearly visible, and specific verbal reference is made to the standards that students are expected to understand.

- Connections are explicitly made with learning standards presented in previous and subsequent lessons (i.e., this lesson does not occur in isolation).

Characteristic 1.2: Exemplars

Characteristic:

Exemplars demonstrate expectations of student achievement.

Indicators:

- Students have concrete examples/models of high quality products (teacher-generated, student-generated or both) that represent mastery of the learning standard(s).

- Students have descriptions, written or oral, in age-appropriate language, of what constitutes a high quality product (e.g., a descriptive rubric).

II. Organization of the Lesson

Characteristic 2.1: Lesson Well-Planned and Organized

Characteristic:

The lesson is well planned and organized. The objectives of the lesson are clearly stated and connected with the learning standards of the larger unit of which it is a part. The lesson develops in a clear, logical manner.

Indicators:

- ***Content and Language objectives are explicit.***
- The plan for the day appears in writing, in age-appropriate language (e.g., an agenda).
- There is a logical flow to the lesson, ***with access for Limited English Proficient students to participate meaningfully in learning activities and fulfill assigned tasks.***
- Lesson objectives are communicated verbally, ***visually*** and/or in writing in age-appropriate language.
- All components of the lesson (learning activities, homework, assessment, etc.) contribute to the lesson objectives and to mastery of the standard(s).
- ***The lesson builds upon everyday language to introduce formal academic English.***
- ***Instruction is delivered using language (vocabulary, sentence structures) that is comprehensible to students, building toward formal academic English.***

Characteristic 2.2: Time Used Effectively and Purposefully

Characteristic:

Time is used efficiently and purposefully.

- Students begin doing math work soon after class begins.
- Students follow classroom routines well enough that minimal time is spent on receiving directions.
- Minimal time is spent on organizational details (attendance, distribution of supplies, etc.).
- Time spent on homework supports the lesson.
- The majority of class time is spent developing new knowledge.
- More student time is spent actively engaging in mathematics than passively receiving instruction about mathematics.
- Sufficient time is allotted to conclude the lesson in a meaningful, appropriate way.

Characteristic 2.3: Multiple Grouping Strategies

Characteristic:

Multiple grouping strategies are used to achieve the learning that is the object of the lesson (e.g., individual, small groups, whole class, teacher-student).

Indicators:

- Possible grouping configurations *(expect to observe two or three):*
    - Part of the lesson involves the entire class.
    - Part of the lesson involves small groups.
    - Part of the lesson involves students working in pairs.
    - Part of the lesson involves students working individually.
- Each configuration and composition of groups is appropriate for the task to be accomplished.
    - ***At times, Limited English Proficient students may use primary language to support access to math (e.g., for clarification of content, to allow increased opportunities for interaction), as a bridge to connecting conceptual understanding in academic English.***
- There are clear guidelines and expectations for group work.
- All groups are supported as they extend their ability to learn and do mathematics.

III. Classroom Environment

Characteristic 3.1: Safe Environment

Characteristic:

It is clear that the students appear to feel safe and are willing to take risks.

Indicators:

- Positive, respectful relationships are evident within the classroom (teacher – student, student – student).
- ***Established routines make expectations clear to students.***
- Expectations about supportive learning relationships are explicit.
- All communication within the classroom is respectful and appropriate.
- The dynamics of the classroom support risk-taking in mathematical discourse, in which students question and contribute and collaborate throughout the lesson.

Characteristic 3.2: Physical Organization

Characteristic:

The appearance and physical organization of the classroom contribute to a positive learning environment.

Indicators:

- Student work is displayed demonstrating writing and problem solving related to the mathematics standards.
- The space is physically arranged as an efficient, functional environment.
- The desk/table arrangement allows for teacher mobility/accessibility.
- The desk/table arrangement allows for a variety of activities.
- The climate of the room (temperature, air quality, light, cleanliness) is conducive to education.

IV. Student Learning

Characteristic 4.1: Student Engagement

Characteristic:

Students are actively engaged in all aspects of the lesson. Behavior is appropriate for the lesson/activities.

Indicators:

- Verbal and non-verbal cues indicate student engagement (e.g., questions, responses, eye contact, attentiveness, posture).
- Students have and utilize required materials (e.g., textbook, homework, pencil).
- Students follow directions and accomplish all assigned tasks.
- Inappropriate behavior is reasonably addressed consistently.
- Students are focused on mathematics throughout the lesson.
- Conversation is on-task and appropriate.
- Students demonstrate respect for property and materials.
- ***Teacher uses awareness of cultural differences to address issues that may preclude students from interacting in ways typically considered productive (e.g., social norms regarding eye contact, questioning teachers) with the goal of teaching students norms of an American classroom.***

Characteristic 4.2: Various Ways of Learning

Characteristic:

Students are engaged in understanding and learning mathematics in various ways that include skill building, conceptual understanding, applying multiple problem-solving strategies, and real-world applications.

Indicators (expect to see two or three):

- Students learn and practice mathematical skills, facts, procedures and algorithms.
- Students explore and discuss mathematical concepts.
- Students use problem-solving strategies.
- Students learn mathematics in the context of real-world problems and applications.

Characteristic 4.3: Students Examine Thinking and Support Reasoning

Characteristic:

Students consciously examine their thinking by questioning their understanding of the mathematics presented. Students support and defend their reasoning with data while using appropriate mathematical language.

Indicators:

- ***Student interactions in a variety of contexts support the development of both mathematical (formal academic) and everyday language.***

- Students support their reasoning with data and evidence.

- Students apply algorithms purposefully in problem-solving situations.

- Students develop multiple problem-solving strategies.

- Students use mathematical language that includes vocabulary related to the lesson.

- Students demonstrate and articulate their mathematical reasoning.

- Student questions and comments indicate mathematical reflection, understanding and development.

V. Teaching

Characteristic 5.1: Content Knowledge

Characteristic:

Depth of content knowledge is evident throughout the presentation of the lesson. Mathematical concepts are presented accurately.

Indicators:

- All mathematics explained and demonstrated throughout the lesson is sound and accurate.

- Mathematical concepts and ideas are explained in multiple ways to enable student understanding.

- Mathematical connections are made across ideas and strands.

- Mathematics is presented as a system of ideas, concepts and understandings, not simply as unrelated procedures, facts and algorithms.

Characteristic 5.2: Probing Questions

Characteristic:

Through the use of probing questions and student responses, decisions are made about what direction to take, what to emphasize, and what to extend in order to build students' mathematical understanding.

Indicators:

- Questions require more than one-word responses.
- ***Teacher allows sufficient time for students to process input and formulate their responses.***
- The level of student understanding, evidenced by student responses, directs how the discussion moves.
- Questions scaffold progression to higher levels of mathematical thinking.
- ***Probing questions are used and student work is examined to assess student understanding with respect to language and math content.***

Characteristic 5.3: Students' Prior Knowledge

Characteristic:

Students' prior knowledge is incorporated as new mathematics concepts are introduced. When students raise comments, questions, and/or concerns, their perspectives are acknowledged and either redirected or affirmed, linking existing knowledge to new knowledge gained within the lesson.

Indicators:

- The lesson requires students to draw upon their existing knowledge of mathematics.
- Students draw on their existing knowledge and their experience of the world around them to inform their learning.
- Students are given time and opportunity to express their understandings and ideas, which are discussed respectfully and used to scaffold learning.
- Connections are explicitly made between students' prior mathematical knowledge and the new ideas being introduced in the lesson, ***including culturally related conventions and algorithms (e.g., use of comma vs. decimal point).***
- ***Cognates are used to provide students access to concepts (e.g., equal-igual, to estimate-estimar, capacity-la capacidad).***

Characteristic 5.4: Student Misconceptions

Characteristic:

Student misconceptions are anticipated/identified and addressed.

Indicators:

- Student misconceptions are anticipated and addressed, ***including language-based misconceptions. (E.g., In a mathematical context, the question: "Does this work for any triangle?" actually means: "Does this work for all triangles?")***

- As misconceptions are identified, students are respectfully redirected to develop accurate mathematical thinking and understanding.

- Students are provided opportunities to identify and correct their own misconceptions through mathematical exploration and discussion.

- Students respectfully correct each other's misconceptions.

Characteristic 5.5: Multiple Forms of Representation

Characteristic:

Classroom strategies incorporate multiple forms of representation (e.g., pictures, words, symbols, diagrams, tables, graphs).

Indicators:

- Mathematical content is expressed in multiple ways (e.g., pictures, words, symbols, diagrams, tables, graphs).

- Opportunities are provided for students to understand that various representations may all express the same mathematical concept.

- Teacher provides opportunities for students to use multiple representations as they develop and explain mathematical ideas.

- ***Key words are introduced and reinforced throughout the lesson.***

VI. Technology

Characteristic 6.1: Instructional Tools

Characteristic:

Appropriate tools for learning are provided (e.g., measuring instruments, manipulatives, calculators, computers). All necessary resources for the lesson are easily accessible. Instruction and support are provided for use of tools.

Indicators:

- All tools appropriate for the lesson are available in sufficient quantity to students (e.g., measuring instruments, manipulatives, calculators and computers).

- Learning tools are easily accessible and functional.

- Use of manipulatives and technology are connected to the lesson objectives (i.e., the technology is not used for its own sake).

- Students are given sufficient instruction and support regarding the use of learning tools.

VII. Equity

Characteristic 7.1: High Expectations for All Students

Characteristic:

There are high learning expectations for all students. All students participate, and their ideas are valued. The belief is evident among all in the classroom that effort, not innate ability, is the key to significant mathematical learning.

Indicators:

- All students are expected to become proficient in the standard(s) addressed in the lesson.
  - *Amplify and enrich the learning experience without simplifying the language of the classroom, to give students more opportunities to learn the concepts involved.*
- Students with special needs are supported as appropriate (e.g., as outlined in IEP).
- All students, regardless of current knowledge, are provided entry into the lesson enabling mathematical learning.
- Wait-time is used effectively to allow all students meaningful participation.
- Students are provided with opportunities to experience achievement through the application of effective effort.

Characteristic 7.2: Variety of Learning Experiences

Characteristic:

Various learning experiences are provided that are appropriate for the range of learners in the classroom (i.e., differentiation by content, process, and/or product).

Indicators:

- Students engage in appropriate activities in terms of complexity and pacing for their current level of understanding and skill, but which challenge them to move forward.
- Students are given opportunities to relate their personal and academic interests to their learning of mathematics.
- Mathematics is presented to students in ways that are responsive to individual learning styles and ways of knowing.
- *Multiple representations are used to provide access to content for English Language Learners (e.g., communication through movement, gestures, visuals, music).*

VIII. Assessment

Characteristic 8.1: Multiple Types of Ongoing Assessment

Characteristic:

There is evidence of multiple types (e.g., group/individual presentations, written reflections, tests) of diagnostic and ongoing formative assessment.

Indicators:

- Data from continuous assessment is used to inform instruction.
- Understanding is assessed through:
    - Student responses to questions
    - Group interactions
    - Student work
    - Student/group presentations
    - Journals/written-reflections
    - Student projects
    - Tests and quizzes
- *Students are provided opportunities to express understanding of mathematics in ways appropriate for their language proficiency (e.g., visual, gestures).*

Characteristic 8.2: Student Ownership of Learning

Characteristic:

Students are engaged in and responsible for their own learning, examining their results with directive feedback that enables revision and improvement.

Indicators:

- Students take initiative to develop and further their own mathematical learning.
- Students receive information (from teacher or other students) that helps them understand their level of mastery regarding the standard(s).
- Students receive direct feedback to explicitly guide continuous progress toward mastery of the standard(s).
- Students are given opportunities to revise their work.

Appendix B
A Shared Vision of Effective Teaching and Learning of K–8 Mathematics in the Jefferson County Public Schools

Source: Jefferson County Teachers Association, 2007. Used with permission.

An effective and coherent mathematics program should be *guided* by a clear set of content standards, but it must be *grounded* in a clear and shared vision of teaching and learning—the two critical reciprocal actions that link teachers and students and largely determine educational impact. While curriculum, materials, professional development, assessment and cultivating broad programmatic support are all necessary components of the educational enterprise, they have little real impact unless they are effectively enacted in each and every classroom where learning is facilitated, supported and maximized.

Accordingly, to ground and guide the development and implementation of a highly effective school mathematics program for *all* students, we describe a research-based vision of teaching and learning with twelve interrelated characteristics of effective instruction in mathematics. It is hoped that this vision will define and inspire excellence in every Jefferson County Public Schools classroom where mathematics is taught and learned.

Effective mathematics instruction is thoughtfully planned. An effective lesson provides multiple opportunities for student learning and must be carefully planned. The days of minimalist lesson plans like "examples 1 and 2 on page 154" or "lesson 6–4: vocabulary, discussion, practice, homework" do not adequately reflect the demands and expectations teachers face. Rather, prior to teaching a lesson, teachers should be empowered and expected to:

- have a clear understanding of the specific learning expectations for their students and how and where these expectations fit in to the larger instructional unit;

- select and try out the set of problems, tasks and/or activities that support the specific learning expectations;

- identify a set of key questions and considered the required explanations that support the problems, tasks and/or activities to be used;

- consider the likely errors that students are likely to make and misconceptions that students are likely to have, and prepare strategies that address these errors and misconceptions; and

- identify the means by which the degree of student learning will be determined.

The heart of effective mathematics instruction is an emphasis on problem solving, reasoning, and sense-making. Nearly every survey of business and industry addresses the critical need for current and prospective workers to be able to reason, question and solve problems. Thus the focus on problem solving as the heart of mathematics and on inquiry as the heart of science are societal, as well as educational, imperatives. However, beyond just rhetoric, effective instruction must consistently include opportunities for students to formulate questions and problems, make hypotheses and conjectures, gather and analyze data, and draw and justify conclusions. This is why students in effective classrooms regularly encounter questions like "why?," "how do you know?," "can you explain that?"

Effective mathematics instruction balances and blends conceptual understanding and procedural skills. Real mathematical literacy is as much about understanding the concept of division, knowing when and why to divide, and being able to interpret the meaning of a remainder as it is about merely knowing how to use an algorithm to find a quotient. Too often, the focus of instruction is on the one right way to get a single right answer, at the expense of understanding why this is the appropriate mathematics, how it relates to other mathematics, and when such mathematics should be used. For this reason, effective instruction balances a focus on conceptual understanding (e.g., the meaning of area and perimeter and how they are related) with a focus on procedural skill (e.g., how to find the area and perimeter of plane figures).

Effective mathematics instruction relies on alternative approaches and multiple representations. At nearly any moment in nearly any class, we know that many students are not processing the content in the way the teacher is processing the content. For example the teacher may be visualizing "three-quarters" as three out of four slices of a small pizza, while one student "sees" three quarters or 75 cents, another student "sees" three red balloons out of a total of four, and still another student "sees" three-quarters of an inch on a ruler. Effective instruction recognizes that students conceptualize mathematical and scientific concepts in different, but often equally appropriate, ways. Effective instruction incorporates deliberate attention to such multiple representations, including concrete materials, and to alternative approaches to accommodate the diverse learning styles within every class.

Effective mathematics instruction uses contexts and connections to engage students and increase the relevance of what is being learned. Teachers have a choice. They can rely on abstractions and rules that are rarely connected to realistic situations or common contexts and ask students the equivalent of finding F when S = 81 in the function F = 4 (S − 65) + 10. Or teachers can take these abstractions and embed them in realistic contexts and problem situations that bring the mathematics and science to life. In this example, telling students that the speeding fine in a particular state is "$4 for every mile per hour over the 65 mph speed limit plus a $10 handling fee for the Police Department" and asking first for the fine when a driver is going 81 mph and then determining a driver's speed if they received a fine of $102. Then consider using a graphing calculator or computer software to represent this function in a table and a graph as well as symbolically, showing where and how the "point" (81, 74) exists within each representation.

Effective mathematics instruction provides frequent opportunities for students to communicate their reasoning and engage in productive discourse. The active, engaged, thinking classroom is a classroom of questions and answers, of inquiries and explanations, of conjectures and justifications, and of written and oral discourse. We know that writing helps to clarify our thinking and that teaching another strengthens our own learning. That is why effective classrooms are often vibrant environments of student communication in the form of explanations, dialogues, arguments and presentations.

Effective mathematics instruction incorporates on-going cumulative review. Almost no one masters something new after one or two lessons and one or two homework assignments. That is why one of the most effective strategies for fostering mastery and retention of critical skills is daily, cumulative review at the beginning of every lesson. Teachers do this as part of a daily warm-up or as "bell-work" that focuses on recent instruction or as a daily "mini-quiz" containing 4 to 6 problems that keep skills sharp, review vocabulary and reinforce conceptual understanding.

Effective mathematics instruction employs technology to enhance learning. Calculators, computers and scientific instruments are increasingly important tools for supporting learning and making instruction more relevant. Graphing calculators that link symbolic, tabular and graphical representations of functions help students develop critical understandings of algebra. Geometry software and scientific simulation software enable students to create mathematical and scientific environments and analyze the impact of changes in selected conditions. Electronic blackboards significantly enhance the impact of such software. But it is not the mere use of technology that enhances learning, any more than it is the use of manipulative materials that "teach." Rather, it is the appropriate, planned and deliberate use of technology to support the development of mathematical understanding that impacts learning.

Effective mathematics instruction maximizes time on task. Videos of classes are striking in their variation in the number of minutes of engaged time on task, that is, the use of time for activities that engage learners and support learning. Some classes begin even before the bell rings with warm-up work posted or distributed at the door, use efficient and established routines to go over homework, transition smoothly from one segment of the lesson to another, keep the focus on student work and student thinking for extended periods of time, are rarely interrupted, do not confuse class work with homework, and still allocate time to building positive relationships with students. In this way, a 45 minute class can easily provide more than 40 minutes of engaged time on task. Other classes, when observed or captured on videotape reveal as much as 20 or more minutes frittered away with organizational matters, frequent interruptions, poor transitions and off-task chatter.

Effective mathematics instruction uses multiple forms of assessment and uses the results of this assessment to adjust instruction. When our focus shifts from what was taught to what was learned, the focus must also shift to assessing what has been learned. While tests and quizzes will continue to be important components of assessment, it is how the results of these quizzes and tests are used to assess the impact of teaching, plan reteaching, prepare individual instruction and design additional diagnosis that translates assessment into better teaching and learning. In addition, effective teachers use observations, class work, projects, and similar vehicles to monitor the quality of learning. Finally, the results of a carefully aligned system of unit tests and end of grade and end of course assessments are regularly analyzed to make curricular and instructional modifications.

Effective mathematics instruction integrates the characteristics of this vision to ensure student mastery of grade-level standards. The often elusive goal of assisting all students to achieve mastery requires a coherent and supportive program that aligns a vision, a set of standards, instructional resources, assessments, collegial sharing and professional development. Moving from mastery by some to truly ensuring mastery by all requires shifts in mind-sets to align with this vision, shifts in curriculum expectations, shifts in instructional practices, and shifts in allocations of resources. It requires a deep commitment to quality and a non-negotiable belief that all students can learn mathematics.

Effective teachers of mathematics reflect on their teaching, individually and collaboratively, and make revisions to enhance student learning. Finally, effective teachers replay their instruction, reflect on what appeared to work and what was more problematic, and examine student responses and work as part of an ongoing cycle of plan—teach—reflect—refine and plan all over again. Moreover, effective teachers work collaboratively with colleagues on issues of the mathematics embedded in the instructional tasks that are used, the pedagogical features of the instruction we conduct, and the student learning evidenced by analysis of student work.

On the one hand, we know with certainty that the elements of this vision do not get implemented by exhortation. We know that people will not do what they cannot envision and cannot do what they do not understand. And we know that the lack of a clear and shared vision commonly results in incoherent, often conflicting, policies and a widely shared perception that "this too will pass."

On the other hand, we also know that once a broadly shared understanding and acceptance of the elements of this vision of effective teaching and learning are in place, school districts, schools, teachers and parents then have a common platform upon which to organize, structure and improve a high quality mathematics program.

Appendix C
Tools

The tools provided in this appendix are available to mathematics leaders and teams of leaders to improve and guide instruction and assessment, and to assist in the development of collaborative teams and support professional learning.

Lesson-Planning Tool

A lesson-planning tool like figure C.1 supports the vision of instruction for your school or district and can be a useful team tool as teachers discuss daily lesson construction that will include the Standards for Mathematical Practice (NGA & CCSSO, 2010; see also page 28). As Kanold (2012b) and his colleagues explain, "The template provides an intentional focus on differentiated instructional planning, Mathematical Practice development, and building the lesson around meaningful student tasks that are engaging and require communication" (p. 59).

Unit: Date: Lesson:		
Learning target: As a result of today's class, students will be able to _____.		
Formative assessment: How will students be expected to demonstrate mastery of the learning target during in-class checks for understanding?		
Probing Questions for Differentiation on Mathematical Tasks		
Assessing Questions (Create questions to scaffold instruction for students who are "stuck" during the lesson or the lesson tasks.)	**Advancing Questions** (Create questions to further learning for students who are ready to advance beyond the standard during class.)	
Mathematical Practice: Which Mathematical Practice will be targeted for proficiency development during this lesson?		
Tasks (Tasks can vary from lesson to lesson.)	**What Will the Teacher Be Doing?** (How will the teacher present and then monitor student response to the task?)	**What Will the Students Be Doing?** (How will students be actively engaged in each part of the lesson?)
Beginning-of-Class Routines How does the warm-up activity connect to students' prior knowledge, or how is it based on analysis of homework?		
Task 1 How will the students be engaged in understanding the learning targets?		

Task 2 How will the task develop student sense making and reasoning?		
Task 3 How will the task require student conjectures and communication?		
Closure How will student questions and reflections be elicited in the summary of the lesson? How will students' understanding of the learning target be determined?		

Materials needed: _____ Technology tips: _____

Figure C.1: CCSS Mathematical Practices lesson-planning tool.
Source: Adapted from Kanold, 2012a. Used with permission.

Regardless of the textbook or course materials, the lesson content, or unit standards for teachers to address, this template provides consistent planning for the "how to" of the lesson, focused on the Standards for Mathematical Practice. The intention is for teachers to use this planning tool in conjunction with other lesson-planning tools that may be provided by the school district (Kanold, 2012b). For example, because this tool is focused on mathematical practices, it does not include lesson components such as independent practice or homework. The lesson design process should involve all teachers of a particular subject and should include thoughtful analytical questions about how students think and learn. Under the guidance of a teacher leader or grade-level or department chair, the teacher team can collaborate during the unit of instruction to design effective mathematics lessons that consider the some of the design elements listed in the tool such as lesson context, lesson process, introduction of the lesson, daily review and closure, and homework.

Five Common Approaches to Conducting Effective Formative Assessment

Teachers can use the following five formative assessment strategies as part of daily lesson planning. Regular use of formative assessment strategies requires that the teacher think differently about teaching and assessment as the focus shifts to learning.

1. Warm-up or bell-ringer items: Teachers often spend the first five minutes of most class periods checking roll and tending to logistical class needs, not teaching. With bell-ringer items, as students enter the classroom, teachers display a small sampling of content from previous lessons, review, a pretest, or a preview on the board or screen. Students work on these items while the teacher is busy taking attendance and so on. An analysis of these items provides the teacher with information regarding students' retention and current understanding or the need for additional instruction.

2. Exit slips: Like the first five minutes, the last five minutes of a class period are also frequently missed instructional opportunities. Exit slips give students one last time to show what they have learned during the day's lesson and allow the teacher to see where they need to give additional instruction. Teachers hand out exit slips about five minutes before the end of class. Students return them to the teacher as they exit the classroom or as they move to another activity. Teachers can also use exit slips to present a specific problem and ask students to reflect on their progress toward the solution.

3. Formative assessment questioning: Too often, the teacher only gets a yes or no answer from one student in the class rather than comprehensive participation from all students. Further, the teacher may not know if that one student just guessed the answer or really understands the concept. Effective teachers ask questions that require thoughtful planning and have the potential to reveal student thinking. These questions probe for understanding or ask students to summarize, evaluate, contrast, or compare. Utilizing such higher-order questions requires teachers to be skilled at facilitating partner, small-group, and whole-class discussions.

4. Simultaneous response techniques: There are also a variety of simultaneous response techniques that allow teachers to receive a response from all students simultaneously. Technology can be a valuable resource, as seen, for example, in the use of *clickers*. Students manage their own clickers or hand-held devices, which allow them to answer at the same time. The hand-held device technology collects and reports all student responses to the teacher instantaneously, allowing for immediate feedback and data collection. Classrooms that have networks for hand-held graphing calculators can collect student work and display a summary of student responses on the screen. Teachers and students can immediately evaluate the class response.

   Students can give a thumbs-up or thumbs-down and use small, individual whiteboards to quickly agree or disagree or respond yes or no. Teachers can observe and assess student actions and dialogue as they are engaged in individual or group work. The purpose of teacher observation of student learning and the simultaneous response technique is to help the teacher understand student thinking. Teachers can ask probing questions to further assess understanding and to encourage deeper thought among students. The teacher can keep notes as he or she observes student thinking to inform instructional decisions.

5. Student summaries: As students work on projects or problem-based activities, teachers can reserve the last few minutes of class to summarize the activity. The teacher can select different groups to share their findings, strategies, representations, and solutions. Depending on the type of daily lesson or the classroom structure, the teacher might ask students randomly to share their findings or summaries, or the teacher might collect written work from all students as a formative assessment check.

Three Intensification Strategies That Make a Difference

Intensification strategies support learning needs of students and are key features found in highly effective schools. Teachers use intensification to offer supportive conditions for students regarding instruction and assessment. Use of intensification strategies indicates that school leaders have made significant changes in time, facility usage, human resources, and fiscal resources in order to provide additional support for student learning. Many students need more time for individual help or for group sessions during which students can exchange mathematics ideas with each other. The following three strategies include offering daily help sessions outside the classroom, extending class time within the school day, and offering preparatory classes to ready students for the next level of learning.

Strategy One: Offering Daily Outside-the-Classroom Help

One of the most straightforward but powerful and effective strategies is to ensure students daily, easy access to help outside of class. In *Mathematics Education at Highly Effective Schools That Serve the Poor: Strategies for Change*, Richard Kitchen, Julie DePree, Sylvia Celédon-Pattichis, and Jonathan Brinkerhoff (2007) list this type of supplemental support for students as a key feature found at the highly effective schools. This strategy offers opportunities for additional learning time with tutors at *multiple* times throughout the school day, including before classes begin (thirty to forty minutes), during the school day (teacher office hours and at lunch times), after school (with late bus transportation provided), and on Saturdays. These high-achieving schools prefer tutoring structures where students receive out-of-class help from their regular mathematics teachers. However, some schools also make tutoring available through partnerships with local university students. In addition, some schools leverage additional tutoring opportunities within daily homeroom and study hall periods with teachers who may or may not be mathematics teachers.

When the school uses nonmathematics teachers as tutors, mathematics teachers work with their colleagues to provide a framework for effective support, such as general problem-solving strategies and effective-questioning strategies. At the YES College Preparatory School System in Houston, Texas, and at the KIPP Academies located throughout the United States, teachers are given cell phones that students use in the evenings to call for homework help (Kitchen et al., 2007; Paek, 2008a). Teachers in these systems universally commit to actively contributing to students' positive and successful daily school experiences. Schools communicate this commitment to students in a variety of ways, ranging from teachers' presence at tutoring times to slogans displayed throughout the school, such as "Whatever It Takes," "Failure Is Not an Option," and "No Excuses." Teaching and learning are the priority at these schools, and providing access to help outside the classroom communicates this message to students in tangible ways each and every day.

Strategy Two: Extending Class Time

There is a long history of research literature documenting the relationship between time spent learning and achievement. This strategy offers proactive support for teacher-identified learners, with more time for learning upfront. The strength of this powerful strategy is that it supports a successful initial learning experience, building confidence and a sense of efficacy for students. This strategy has the potential to significantly reduce the need for remediation or tutors by replacing the daily sense of failure some students experience with successful learning experiences that come with more time and attention.

High-achieving schools leverage more learning time in one of two general ways. The first is to offer some sections of a course with a longer class period. For example, at Norfolk Public Schools in Norfolk, Virginia, mathematics classes last for a minimum of ninety minutes (Paek, 2008a). In these sections, students have more time to discuss, question, consider, explore, share, practice, and build new mathematical ideas, receiving help with prerequisite concepts and skills from the teacher as needed. The extended learning time helps students develop greater conceptual understanding and confidence with skills. This instruction is distinctly different than a regular lesson with homework help time. A possible downside to this strategy is that it might create a homogeneous group of students and therefore a less rich learning environment if only struggling students participate in the extended learning time (Boaler, 2011). Evanston Township High School in Evanston, Illinois, structures all algebra 1 classes with more time and recruits upper-level students to assist.

The second design format for providing more learning time is to offer students a one-period mathematics support course (typically as a mathematics credit with pass or fail grading), which students take in addition to their regular mathematics class. In this version of the intensification strategy (see page 35), students have more time to build new mathematical ideas and fill in prerequisite skills and concepts. An important distinction in this setting is the extra hour of class time that acts as *preteaching* content. The preteaching gives students sufficient content background and think time needed to enter into and benefit from the challenging heterogeneous learning environment of the regular classroom (Kitchen et al., 2007). At Bellevue School District in Bellevue, Washington, this strategy, along with others such as eliminating secondary tracking based on student ability, allows all students to successfully complete four years of high school mathematics, including precalculus, before they graduate (Paek, 2008b).

Two cautions are cited in case studies that utilize this strategy. First, in both formats, teachers need professional learning time to develop effective ways to use this extended time. Without differentiated instructional strategies and explicit planning, additional learning time can devolve into nothing more than homework help. Secondly, the same teacher should teach the support class and regular mathematics class (optimal), or regular and support-classroom teachers should collaborate and coordinate instruction so that the two classes work together to support learning for students. Offering extended mathematics classes or mathematics support classes may mean fewer electives for students. While this can be a difficult choice, it is a choice that solidly represents a school's and student's commitment to mathematics achievement that schools can embrace for the future payoff of academic success.

When implemented well, this strategy shows promise for helping students meet rigorous mathematics course requirements at elementary, secondary, and university levels (Paek, 2008a). The variable in both versions of this intensification strategy is the amount of time students are given to meet content requirements; mathematics expectations and the level of difficulty are held constant. Both versions attempt to anticipate when students might not be successful in a regular-length class and preempt their failure with a proven support strategy.

Strategy Three: Offering Preparatory Courses

Preparatory courses, or *jumpstart* or *bridge* programs, come in many sizes and types. Typically, schools offer preparatory courses during the summer, but they may also offer them during the school year. These courses provide instruction on content that is somewhat outside the standard K–12 content. In addition to previewing upcoming mathematics topics, these courses address issues like community building, mathematical reasoning, and problem solving, and they reinforce ideas about how students learn and what it takes to learn. They prepare students for success by acknowledging and addressing learner needs that might otherwise lead to poor academic performance. The courses act as a foundation for success at the next level of schooling and are explicitly not remedial programs.

Two such programs that prepare students for success in algebra 1 are Step Up to High School in the Chicago Public Schools and the Academic Youth Development (AYD) program. Research on the effect of social interventions on student engagement and academic success helped develop these programs (Aronson, Fried, & Good, 2002; Good, Aronson, & Inzlicht, 2003; Treisman & Asera, 1990). Both programs have yielded pre- and postsurvey data from students suggesting gains in student confidence and the ability to do well in challenging academic courses (Paek, 2008b).

A third example of bridge courses comes from Eastside College Preparatory School in East Palo Alto, California. Here, the regular school-year curriculum includes courses that help to prepare students for college-level work. The course catalog contains additional academic courses that focus on reasoning and analytical skills and another that prepares students for the demands of independent research and writing.

In all three bridge courses, we see willingness on the part of educators to acknowledge that for students to succeed at the next school level (moving to middle school, high school, or college), they need support to successfully navigate and learn within the new system. For students who need an explicit introduction to a new learning environment, a preparatory class can be the difference between alienation followed by withdrawal and confident forward progress.

Self-Evaluation Rubric for PRIME Assessment Leadership

Principle 4: Ensure timely, accurate monitoring of student learning and adjustment of teacher instruction for improved student learning.

What is my progress on the PRIME indicators for Assessment Leadership? To what extent does my leadership ensure:	STAGE 1 Know and Model				STAGE 2 Collaborate and Implement			
	I have no understanding and have taken no action.	I have a basic understanding.	I have deep understanding.	I use my understanding to take action and model for others.	I develop awareness in others, but often inconsistently.	I ensure collaborative discussion by teams.	I follow up on discussion with collaborative action by teacher teams.	I systematically and intentionally ensure complete implementation by all teachers and teaching teams.
	1	2	3	4	1	2	3	4
1. Every teacher uses student assessments that are congruent and aligned by grade level or course content?								
2. Every teacher uses formative assessment processes to inform teacher practice and student learning?								
3. Every teacher uses summative assessment data to evaluate mathematics grade-level, course, and program effectiveness?								

Source: NCSM, 2008.

Stages of Team Development

While the process of developing a professional learning team may feel uniquely personal, there are certain stages of development common across teams. By understanding that these stages exist—and by describing both the challenges and opportunities inherent in each stage—school leaders can improve the chances of success for every learning team. Use the following quick reference guide to evaluate the stages of team development in your building and to identify practical strategies for offering support.

Characteristics of Stage	Strategies for Offering Support
Stage: Filling the Time	
• Teams ask, "What is it exactly that we're supposed to do together?" • Meetings can ramble. • Frustration levels can be high. • Activities are simple and scattered rather than a part of a coherent plan for improvement.	☐ Set clear work expectations. ☐ Define specific tasks for teams to complete (for example, identifying essential objectives or developing common assessments). ☐ Provide sample agendas and sets of norms to help define work.
Stage: Sharing Personal Practices	
• Teamwork focuses on sharing instructional practices or resources. • A self-imposed standardization of instruction appears. • Less-experienced colleagues benefit from the planning acumen of colleagues. • Teams delegate planning responsibilities.	☐ Require teams to come to consensus around issues related to curriculum, assessment, or instruction. ☐ Require teams to develop shared minilessons delivered by all teachers. ☐ Structure efforts to use student learning data in the planning process. ☐ Ask questions that require data analysis to answer.
Stage: Developing Common Assessments	
• Teachers begin to wrestle with the question, "What does mastery look like?" • Emotional conversations around the characteristics of quality instruction and the importance of individual objectives emerge. • Pedagogical controversy is common.	☐ Provide teams with additional training in interpersonal skills and conflict management. ☐ Moderate or mediate initial conversations around common assessments to model strategies for joint decision making. ☐ Ensure that teams have had training in how to best develop effective common assessments. ☐ Create a library of sample assessments from which teams can draw.

Characteristics of Stage	Strategies for Offering Support
Stage: Analyzing Student Learning	
• Teams begin to ask, "Are students learning what they are supposed to be learning?" • Teams shift attention from a focus on teaching to a focus on learning. • Teams need technical and emotional support. • Teachers publically face student learning results. • Teachers can be defensive in the face of unyielding evidence. • Teachers can grow competitive.	☐ Provide tools and structures for effective data analysis. ☐ Repurpose positions to hire teachers trained in data analysis to support teams new to working with assessment results. ☐ Emphasize a separation of "person" from "practice." ☐ Model a data-oriented approach by sharing results that reflect on the work of practitioners beyond the classroom (for example, by principals, counselors, and instructional resource teachers).
Stage: Differentiating Follow-Up	
• Teachers begin responding instructionally to student data. • Teams take collective action, rather than responding to results as individuals. • Principals no longer direct team development. Instead, they serve as collaborative partners in conversations about learning.	☐ Ask provocative questions about instructional practices and levels of student mastery. ☐ Demonstrate flexibility as teams pursue novel approaches to enrichment and remediation. ☐ Provide concrete ways to support differentiation. ☐ Identify relevant professional development opportunities; allocate funds to after-school tutoring programs. ☐ Redesign positions to focus additional human resources on struggling students.
Stage: Reflecting on Instruction	
• Teams begin to ask, "What instructional practices are most effective with our students?" • Learning is connected back to teaching. • Practitioners engage in deep reflection about instruction. • Action research and lesson study are used to document the most effective instructional strategies for a school's student population.	☐ Facilitate a team's efforts to study the teaching-learning connection. ☐ Create opportunities for teachers to observe one another teaching. ☐ Provide release time for teams to complete independent projects. ☐ Facilitate opportunities for cross-team conversations to spread practices and perspectives across an entire school. ☐ Celebrate and publicize the findings of team studies.

Source: Graham & Ferriter, 2010. Used with permission.

page 2 of 2

References and Resources

■■■■

Aronson, J., Fried, C. B., & Good, C. (2002). Reducing the effects of stereotype threat on African American college students by shaping theories of intelligence. *Journal of Experimental Social Psychology, 38,* 113–125.

Artz, A. F., & Newman, C. M. (1990). *How to use cooperative learning in the mathematics class.* Reston, VA: National Council of Teachers of Mathematics.

Ash, P. B., & D'Auria, J. (2013). *School systems that learn: Improving professional practice, overcoming limitations and diffusing innovation.* Thousand Oaks, CA: Corwin Press.

Battista, M. (1994). Teacher beliefs and the reform movement in mathematics education. *Phi Delta Kappan, 75*(6), 462–463, 466–468, 470.

Black, P., & Wiliam, D. (2001). *Inside the black box: Raising standards through classroom assessments.* London: King's College London School of Education.

Boaler, J. (2011). Changing students' lives through the de-tracking of urban mathematics classrooms. *Journal of Urban Mathematics Education, 4*(1), 7–14. Accessed at http://ed-osprey.gsu.edu/ojs/index.php/JUME/article/viewFile/138/85 on September 11, 2013.

Borko, H. (2004). Professional development and teacher learning: Mapping the terrain. *Educational Researcher, 33*(8), 3–15.

Burke, K. (2010). *Balanced assessment: From formative to summative.* Bloomington, IN: Solution Tree Press.

Campbell, P. (2012). Coaching and elementary mathematics specialists: Findings from research. In J. M. Bay-Williams & W. R. Speer (Eds.), *Professional collaborations in mathematics teaching and learning: Seeking success for all* (pp. 147–160). Reston, VA: National Council of Teachers of Mathematics.

Charles, R. I. (2005). Big ideas and understandings as the foundation for elementary and middle school mathematics. *Journal of Mathematics Education Leadership, 7*(3), 9–24.

Chetty, R., Friedman, J. N., & Rockoff, J. E. (2011). *The long-term impacts of teachers: Teacher value-added and student outcomes in adulthood.* Accessed at http://obs.rc.fas.harvard.edu/chetty/value_added.html on August 25, 2012.

Cooper, C. I. (2011). A concurrent support course for intermediate algebra. *Research and Teaching in Developmental Education, 28*(1), 16–29.

Costa, A. L., & Garmston, R. J. (2002). *Cognitive coaching: A foundation for renaissance schools* (2nd ed.). Norwood, MA: Christopher-Gordon.

Danielson, C. (2007). *Enhancing professional practice: A framework for teaching* (2nd ed.). Alexandria, VA: Association for Supervision and Curriculum Development.

Danielson, C. (2011). *The framework for teaching evaluation instrument.* Princeton, NJ: The Danielson Group.

Darling-Hammond, L., & Adamson, F. (2013). *Developing assessments of deeper learning: The costs and benefits of using tests that help students learn.* Stanford, CA: Stanford Center for Opportunity Policy in Education.

Darling-Hammond, L., Wei, R. C., Andree, A., Richardson, N., & Orphanos, S. (2009). *Professional learning in the learning profession: A status report on teacher development in the United States and abroad.* Dallas, TX: National Staff Development Council.

Dean, C. B., Hubbell, E. R., Pitler, H., & Stone, B. (2012). *Classroom instruction that works: Research-based strategies for increasing student achievement* (2nd ed.). Alexandria, VA: Association for Supervision and Curriculum Development.

Desimone, L. M., Porter, A. C., Garet, M. S., Yoon, K. S., & Birman, B. F. (2001). Effects of professional development on teachers' instruction: Results from a three-year longitudinal study. *Educational Evaluation and Policy Analysis, 24*(2), 81–112.

Domina, T., & Saldana, J. (2012). Does raising the bar level the playing field? Mathematics curricular intensification and inequality in American high schools, 1982–2004. *American Educational Research Journal, 49*(4), 685–708.

Donovan, M. S., & Bransford, J. D. (2005). *How students learn: Mathematics in the classroom.* Washington, DC: National Academies Press.

DuFour, R., DuFour, R., Eaker, R., & Many, T. (2010). *Learning by doing: A handbook for professional learning communities at work* (2nd ed.). Bloomington, IN: Solution Tree Press.

Dweck, C. S. (2006). *Mindset: The new psychology of success.* New York: Random House.

Elmore, R. F., & Burney, D. (1997). Improving instruction through professional development in New York City's Community District #2. *CPRE Policy Bulletin.* Accessed at www.cpre.org/sites/default/files/policybulletin/901_pb-02.pdf on September 11, 2013.

Foster, D. (2007). *Silicon Valley Mathematics Initiative: Pedagogical content coaching.* Palo Alto, CA: Noyce Foundation.

Frey, N., Fisher, D., & Everlove, S. (2009). *Productive group work: How to engage students, build teamwork, and promote understanding.* Alexandria, VA: Association for Supervision and Curriculum Development.

Garmston, R. J., & Wellman, B. M. (2009). *The adaptive school: A sourcebook for developing collaborative groups* (2nd ed.). Norwood, MA: Christopher-Gordon.

Gearhart, M., & Omundson, E. (2008). *Assessment portfolios as opportunities for teacher learning* (CRESST Report 736). Los Angeles: National Center for Research on Evaluation, Standards, and Student Testing.

Goddard, Y. L., Goddard, R. D., & Tschannen-Moran, M. (2007). A theoretical and empirical investigation of teacher collaboration for school improvement and student achievement in public elementary schools. *Teachers College Record, 109*(4), 877–896.

Goldsby, D. S., & Cozza, B. (2002). Writing samples to understand mathematical thinking. *Mathematics Teaching in the Middle School, 7*(9), 517–520.

Good, C., Aronson, J., & Inzlicht, M. (2003). Improving adolescents' standardized test performance: An intervention to reduce the effects of stereotype threat. *Journal of Applied Developmental Psychology, 24,* 645–662.

Graham, P., & Ferriter, W. (2010). *Building a Professional Learning Community at Work™.* Bloomington, IN: Solution Tree Press.

Greenberg, J., & Walsh, K. (2012). *What teacher preparation programs teach about K–12 assessment: A review.* Accessed at www.nctq.org/dmsView/What_Teacher_Prep_Programs_Teach_K-12_Assessment_NCTQ_Report on September 11, 2013.

Guskey, T. R. (1986). Staff development and the process of teacher change. *Educational Researcher, 15*(4), 5–12.

Hauk, S., Deon, R., Judd, A. B., Kreps, J., & Novak, J. (2009). *No teacher left behind: Pedagogical content knowledge and mathematics teacher professional development.* Manuscript submitted for review. Accessed at www.mathsci.unco.edu/hauk/papers/HaukMSPpaperMATH.pdf on September 10, 2013.

Herman, J., & Linn, R. (2013). *On the road to assessing deeper learning: The status of Smarter Balanced and PARCC assessment consortia* (CRESST Report 823). Los Angeles: National Center for Research on Evaluation, Standards, and Student Testing.

Hiebert, J. (1999). Relationships between research and the NCTM standards. *Journal for Research in Mathematics Education, 30*(1), 3–19.

Hill, H. C., Ball, D. L., & Schilling, S. G. (2008). Unpacking pedagogical content knowledge: Conceptualizing and measuring teachers' topic-specific knowledge of students. *Journal for Research in Mathematics Education, 39*(4), 372–400.

Hill, H. C., Rowan, B., & Ball, D. L. (2005). Effects of teachers' mathematical knowledge for teaching on student achievement. *American Educational Research Journal, 42*(2), 371–406.

Hoffer, W. (2012). *Minds on mathematics: Using math workshop to develop deep understanding in grades 4–8.* Portsmouth, NH: Heinemann.

Hoyles, C. (1992). Mathematics teaching and mathematics teachers: A meta-case study. *For the Learning of Mathematics, 12*(3), 32–44.

Hull, T. H., Balka, D. S., & Miles, R. H. (2009). *A guide to mathematics coaching: Processes for increasing student achievement.* Thousand Oaks, CA: Corwin Press.

Hull, T. H., Miles, R. H., & Balka, D. S. (2012). *The Common Core mathematics standards: Transforming practice through team leadership.* Thousand Oaks, CA: Corwin Press.

Jefferson County Teachers Association. (2007). *A shared vision of effective teaching and learning of K-8 mathematics in the Jefferson County Public Schools.* Accessed at http://frameweld-workshop.s3.amazonaws.com/files/4f5e004c0c1c44d876000125/4f5e00920c1c440277000094/4f5e06060c1c444508000002/13_leinwald_2_of_3/2012/03/12/13_leinwald_2_of_3.pdf on December 20, 2013.

Joyner, J., & Muri, M. (2011). *INFORMative assessment: Formative assessment to improve math achievement.* Sausalito, CA: Math Solutions.

Kanold, T. D. (Ed.). (2012a). *Common Core mathematics in a PLC at Work, high school.* Bloomington, IN: Solution Tree Press.

Kanold, T. D. (Ed.). (2012b). *Common Core mathematics in a PLC at Work, leaders guide.* Bloomington, IN: Solution Tree Press.

Kanold, T. D. (Ed.). (2013). *Common Core mathematics in a PLC at Work, grades 6–8.* Bloomington, IN: Solution Tree Press.

Kanold, T. D., Briars, D. J., & Fennell, F. (2012). *What principals need to know about teaching and learning mathematics.* Bloomington, IN: Solution Tree Press.

Keeley, P., & Tobey, C. R. (2011). *Mathematics formative assessment: 75 practical strategies for linking assessment, instruction, and learning.* Thousand Oaks, CA: Corwin Press.

Kilpatrick, J., Swafford, J., & Findell, B. (Eds.). (2001). *Adding it up: Helping children learn mathematics.* Washington, DC: National Academies Press.

Kitchen, R. S., DePree, J., Celédon-Pattichis, S., & Brinkerhoff, J. (2007). *Mathematics education at highly effective schools that serve the poor: Strategies for change.* Mahwah, NJ: Erlbaum.

Knight, J. (2007). *Instructional coaching: A partnership approach to improving instruction.* Thousand Oaks, CA: Corwin Press.

Lambert, L. (2002). Leading the conversations. In L. Lambert (Ed.), *The constructivist leader* (2nd ed., pp. 63–88). New York: Teachers College Press.

Leinwand, S. (n.d.). *High leverage mathematics instruction practices.* Accessed at steveleinwand.com /wp-content/uploads/2012/09/High-Leverage-Mathematics-Instruction-Practices.docx on January 2, 2014.

Leinwand, S. (2009). *Accessible mathematics: 10 instructional shifts that raise student achievement.* Portsmouth, NH: Heinemann.

Leinwand, S. (2011). *Moving beyond typical professional development that doesn't work and toward effective teacher development that can make a real difference.* Accessed at www.mathedleadership.org/docs /resources/materials/2011/NCSM11-122_Leinwand.pdf on December 31, 2013.

Leinwand, S. (2012). *Sensible mathematics: A guide for school leaders in the era of Common Core State Standards* (2nd ed.). Portsmouth, NH: Heinemann.

Lipton, L. (2011). *Groups at work: Strategies and structures for professional learning.* Sherman, CT: MiraVia.

Little, J. W. (1990). The persistence of privacy: Autonomy and initiative in teachers' professional relations. *Teachers College Record, 91*(4), 509–536.

Loucks-Horsley, S., Hewson, P. W., Love, N., & Stiles, K. E. (1998). *Designing professional development for teachers of science and mathematics.* Thousand Oaks, CA: Corwin Press.

Loucks-Horsley, S., Love, N., Stiles, K. E., Mundry, S., & Hewson, P. W. (2003). *Designing professional development for teachers of science and mathematics* (2nd ed.). Thousand Oaks, CA: Corwin Press.

Lynch School of Education. (n.d.). *TIMSS 1995 database.* Accessed at http://timss.bc.edu/timss1995i /Database.html on January 2, 2014.

Ma, L. (2010). *Knowing and teaching elementary mathematics: Teachers' understanding of fundamental mathematics in China and the United States* (2nd ed.). New York: Routledge.

Martin, T. S. (Ed.). (2007). *Mathematics teaching today: Improving practice, improving student learning* (2nd ed.). Reston, VA: National Council of Teachers of Mathematics.

Marzano, R. J., & Pickering, D. (2011). *The highly engaged classroom.* Bloomington, IN: Marzano Research Laboratory.

Massachusetts Department of Elementary and Secondary Education. (2009). *Characteristics of a standards-based mathematics classroom.* Accessed at www.doe.mass.edu/omste/news07/mathclass_char.pdf on September 12, 2013.

McCallum, W. G., Black, A., Umland, K., & Whitesides, E. (n.d.). [Common Core Mathematical Practices model]. Accessed at http://commoncoretools.files.wordpress.com/2011/03/practices.pdf on October 28, 2012.

Means, B. (2008). *Levers for improving mathematics learning in high-poverty high schools.* Menlo Park, CA: SRI International.

Moses, R., & Cobb, C. (2001). *Radical equations: Math literacy and civil rights.* Boston: Beacon Press.

National Center for Education Statistics. (n.d.). *Trends in International Mathematics and Science Study (TIMSS)—TIMSS 2011 results.* Accessed at nces.ed.gov/results11.asp on December 30, 2013.

National Council of Supervisors of Mathematics. (1998). *Improving student achievement through designated district and school mathematics program leaders.* Accessed at http://ncsmonline.org/NCSM Publications/position.html#positiontop on October 23, 2013.

National Council of Supervisors of Mathematics. (2007). *Improving student achievement by leading effective and collaborative teams of mathematics teachers.* Accessed at https://gippslandtandlcoaches .wikispaces.com/file/view/Improving+Stud.+Achieve.+by+leading+Effective+and+collaborative +teams+of+mathematics+Teachers.pdf on September 11, 2013.

National Council of Supervisors of Mathematics. (2008). *The PRIME leadership framework: Principles and indicators for mathematics education leaders.* Bloomington, IN: Solution Tree Press.

National Council of Supervisors of Mathematics. (2013a). *Improving student achievement by infusing highly effective instructional strategies into RTI tier I instruction.* Denver, CO: Author.

National Council of Supervisors of Mathematics. (2013b). *Improving student achievement in mathematics by using manipulatives with classroom instruction.* Denver, CO: Author.

National Council of Teachers of Mathematics. (1991). *Professional standards for teaching mathematics.* Reston, VA: Author.

National Council of Teachers of Mathematics. (2000). *Principles and standards for school mathematics.* Reston, VA: Author.

National Council of Teachers of Mathematics. (2008). *Equity in mathematics education* [Position paper]. Accessed at www.nctm.org/about/content.aspx?id=39817 on December 19, 2013.

National Governors Association Center for Best Practices & Council of Chief State School Officers. (2010). *Common Core State Standards for mathematics.* Washington, DC: Authors.

No Child Left Behind Act of 2001, Pub. L. No. 107-110, 115 Stat. 1425 (2002).

Paek, P. L. (2008a). Mathematics coaching: Silicon Valley Mathematics Initiative. In *Practices worthy of attention: Local innovations in strengthening secondary mathematics* (pp. 1–5). Austin: Charles A. Dana Center at the University of Texas at Austin.

Paek, P. L. (2008b). Raising student achievement through academic intensification. In *Practices worthy of attention: Local innovations in strengthening secondary mathematics* (pp. 1–11). Austin: Charles A. Dana Center at the University of Texas at Austin.

Parrish, S. (2010). *Number talks: Helping children build mental math and computation strategies, grades K–5.* Sausalito, CA: Math Solutions.

Partnership for Assessment of Readiness for College and Careers. (2013). *PARCC field test administration and timeline.* Accessed at www.parcconline.org/field-test on December 24, 2013.

Peterson, K. D., & Deal, T. E. (1998). How leaders influence the culture of schools. *Educational Leadership, 56*(1), 28–30.

Quint, J. (2011). *Professional development for teachers: What two rigorous studies tell us.* New York: Manpower Development Research.

Ramirez, N. G., & Celédon-Pattichis, S. (Eds.). (2012). *Beyond good teaching: Advancing mathematics education for ELLs*. Reston, VA: National Council of Teachers of Mathematics.

Reys, B. J., & Bay-Williams, J. M. (2003). The role of textbooks in implementing the curriculum principle and the learning principle. *Mathematics Teaching in the Middle School, 9*(2), 120–124.

Reys, B. J., Dingman, S., Sutter, A., & Teuscher, D. (2005). *Development of state-level mathematics curriculum documents: Report of a survey*. Columbia: University of Missouri, Center for the Study of Mathematics Curriculum.

Rohrer, D. (2009). The effects of spacing and mixing practice problems. *Journal for Research in Mathematics Education, 40*(1), 4–17.

Schmidt, W. H., Wang, H. C., & McKnight, C. C. (2005). Curriculum coherence: An examination of U.S. mathematics and science content standards from an international perspective. *Journal of Curriculum Studies, 37*(5), 525–559.

Schmoker, M. (2005). Here and now: Improving teaching and learning. In R. DuFour, R. Eaker, & R. DuFour (Eds.), *On common ground: The power of professional learning communities* (pp. xi–xvi). Bloomington, IN: Solution Tree Press.

Schrock, C., Norris, K., Pugalee, D. K., Scitz, R., & Hollingshead, F. (2013a). *NCSM great tasks for mathematics K–5*. Lakewood, CO: National Council of Supervisors of Mathematics.

Schrock, C., Norris, K., Pugalee, D. K., Seitz, R., & Hollingshead, F. (2013b). *NCSM great tasks for mathematics 6–12*. Lakewood, CO: National Council of Supervisors of Mathematics.

Skott, J. (2001). The emerging practices of a novice teacher: The roles of his school mathematics images. *Journal of Mathematics Teacher Education, 4*(1), 3–28.

Smarter Balanced Assessment Consortium. (2012). *Field test*. Accessed at www.smarterbalanced.org /field-test on December 24, 2013.

Smith, M. S. (2011). *Practice-based professional development for teachers of mathematics*. Reston, VA: National Council of Teachers of Mathematics.

Smith, M. S., & Stein, M. K. (2011). *5 practices for orchestrating productive mathematics discussions*. Reston, VA: National Council of Teachers of Mathematics.

Speer, W. R., & Bay-Williams, J. M. (Eds.). (2012). *Professional collaborations in mathematics teaching and learning: Seeking success for all*. Reston, VA: National Council of Teachers of Mathematics.

Stecher, B. M., Epstein, S., Hamilton, L. S., Marsh, J. A., Robyn, A., McCombs, J. S., et al. (2008). *Pain and gain: Implementing No Child Left Behind in three states, 2004–2006*. Santa Monica, CA: RAND.

Stiff, L. V., & Johnson, J. L. (2011). Mathematical reasoning and sense making begins with the opportunity to learn. In M. E. Strutchens & J. R. Quander (Eds.), *Focus in high school mathematics: Fostering reasoning and sense making for all students*. Reston, VA: National Council of Teachers of Mathematics.

Stiggins, R., Arter, J., Chappuis, J., & Chappuis, S. (2007). *Classroom assessment* for *student learning: Doing it right—using it well* (Special edition). Upper Saddle River, NJ: Pearson.

Stonewater, J. K. (2002). The mathematics writer's checklist: The development of a preliminary assessment tool for writing in mathematics. *School Science and Mathematics, 102*(7), 324–334.

Sztajn, P. (2003). Adapting reform ideas in different mathematics classrooms: Beliefs beyond mathematics. *Journal of Mathematics Teacher Education, 6*(1), 53–75.

Thompson, A. (1992). Teachers' beliefs and conceptions: A synthesis of the research. In D. A. Grouws (Ed.), *Handbook of research on mathematics teaching and learning* (pp. 127–146). New York: Macmillan Library Reference USA.

Treisman, P. U., & Asera, R. (1990). Teaching mathematics to a changing population: The professional development program at the University of California, Berkeley. In N. Fisher, H. Keynes, & P. Wagreich (Eds.), *Mathematics and education reform: Proceedings of the July 6–8, 1988 workshop* (pp. 31–62). Providence, RI: American Mathematical Society.

Van de Walle, J. A., Karp, K. S., & Bay-William, J. M. (2009). *Elementary and middle school mathematics teaching developmentally* (7th ed.). Boston: Allyn & Bacon.

Wellman, B., & Lipton, L. (2004). *Data-driven dialogue: A facilitator's guide to collaborative inquiry.* Sherman, CT: MiraVia.

Weiss, I. (2010, December). *Deepening teacher mathematics content knowledge: What do we know about effective professional development?* [PowerPoint slides]. Presentation for the Conference Board of the Mathematical Sciences, Alexandria, VA.

Weiss, I., & Heck, D. (2010). *Why teachers' mathematics content knowledge matters: A summary of studies.* Raleigh, NC: Horizon Research.

West, L., & Staub, F. (2003). *Content-focused coaching: Transforming mathematics lessons.* Portsmouth, NH: Heinemann.

Wiliam, D. (2011). *Embedded formative assessment.* Bloomington, IN: Solution Tree Press.

Index

■■■■